A Lighthearted T_____t
On a Search for the
Two-Story Outhouse

By

Norman D. Weis

PHOTOGRAPHS BY THE AUTHOR

The CAXTON PRINTERS, Ltd.
Caldwell, Idaho 83605
1988

Library of Congress Cataloging-in-Publication Data

Weis, Norm, 1923-
    A lighthearted tour of the West on a search for the two-story
outhouse / by Norman D. Weis ; photographs by the author.
        p.   cm.
    ISBN 0-87004-326-9 :
    1. Cities and towns, Ruined, extinct, etc.—West (U.S.) 2. Cities
and towns, Ruined, etc.—Canada, Western. 3. West (U.S.)–
–Description and travel—1981- 4. Canada, Western—Description and
travel. 5. Weis, Norm, 1923- —Journeys—West (U.S.) 6. Weis,
Norm, 1923- Journeys—Canada, Western. I. Title.
F595.3.W45   1987
917.8—dc 19   87-35425
                                                                    CIP

Lithographed and bound in the United States of America by
The CAXTON PRINTERS, Ltd.
Caldwell, Idaho 83605
146944

To Mike Herbison
who thought this book should be entitled,
Early American Evacuation

With special thanks to Jon Brady and Len Brakke

Contents

List of Illustrations

Introduction

SEVERAL CONVERSATIONS were bouncing about the faculty lounge at a small college in central Wyoming. When the physics professor mentioned having seen a two-story outhouse, a sudden silence fell over the group. The phrase seemed to hang in the air as a dozen instructors tried to rationalize what seemed to be a conflict of terms. Finally someone weakened.

"Okay, I'll bite. How can an outhouse be two-storied?"

As the physics prof told about his visit to the old town of Dillon, Wyoming, we were all ears, expecting a punch line to crop out somewhere. His explanation, however, was completely serious.

"There wasn't much left in the town except a few tumbled-down log walls, an old safe, and the remains of a number of privies, some built on platforms elevated well above ground. I climbed the dozen or so steps on one that looked solid, and found what remained of an old two-holer."

We bombarded the man with questions: Why was it elevated? Was there a door leading to the lower floor? Was it really two stories? The professor fielded most of the questions, explaining that some outhouses in the town were merely elevated, but others looked like the remains of honest-to-goodness two-story outhouses.

That quieted the group down once more while everyone set to figuring just how such a structure might be designed. I wondered about the fate of some poor soul occupying a seat on the main floor while another made use of the facilities above.

Perhaps, we concluded, the two levels were offset. But the advantages of the two-story configuration remained a mystery.

My curiosity aroused, I determined to travel to Dillon at the first opportunity and have a look for myself. Little did I suspect that this would be the start of a twelve-year search taking me to eleven states and four Canadian provinces.

Old-timers at or near each site I visited always suggested new places to observe unusual outhouses. Many leads were false, owing perhaps to faulty memories, but sometimes I was led down the garden path by reports I now know to be 100 percent fictitious. About one in ten reports was accurate, leading me to grand examples of yesterday's feats of sanitary engineering.

Along with these reports came a multitude of stories, some having little to do with outdoor plumbing. But the stories were as unforgettable as the best double-decker: the engineer who ran his train through a house; the quicksand ford located smack across the middle of the road to town; or the sign mounted on the top level of one two-story outhouse that read: "Anything over eight pounds must be lowered by rope!"

It took many trips to cover all the leads. Upon returning from most of these trips, I would find more suggestions in the mail, many of them for sites near the towns just visited. Eventually, I found dozens of elevated outhouses, and a number of honest-to-goodness two-story outhouses, some of which were still in operation. There were outhouses on high trestles, outhouses hanging over river banks, creek straddlers, leaners, open-air jobs, outhouse-bridge combos, and one fantastic specimen in Calgary, Alberta, featuring a two-door four-holer on top of a four-door eight-holer, the whole thing topped with a cupola, capped in turn with a Canadian flag blowing stiffly in the breeze.

Now, after a dozen years, thousands of miles of travel, and one hundred rolls of film, here is the account of my search for the two-story outhouse.

TWO-STORY OUTHOUSE

Part I – Wyoming

Dillon

THE SMALL ghost town named Dillon lies twenty miles west of Encampment, deep in the Sierra Madre of south central Wyoming. The black-topped road changed to gravel twenty miles short of Dillon, then degenerated to muddy ruts covered with occasional snowbanks. At nine thousand feet above sea level, access to town is possible for just two months each year, and then only by means of four-wheel drive vehicles. A local sheepherder calls the last three mile stretch the "alternate route," and explains, "it alternates between mud a foot deep and boulders a foot high."

It began to rain as I drove along the deserted main street. A search of the town's remains revealed only collapsed log walls, a few criblike structures that looked like the remains of elevated outhouses, and an old rusty safe blown open by some hopeful treasure hunters.

Thoroughly soaked, and muddy to the knees, I headed back to the pickup. Before I could reach it, a jeep pulled up alongside. The driver asked if I needed help. I had to holler to be heard over the sound of the rain.

"Yes, could you tell me if there is an outhouse around here?"

Mouth agape, the driver cranked up the window of the jeep and drove off.

I slipped and bumped my way downhill, back to Encampment, hoping to garner some information from the local old-timers.

Vera Oldman, the leading historian of the town, had for some years undertaken the job of preserving artifacts of the mining era that had brought life to the towns in that area. She was a prime mover in the establishment of the local museum. She hoped to reconstruct one of Dillon's two-story outhouses and perhaps restore one of the many towers that made up the longest tramway in the world, carrying ore sixteen miles from the mine just north of Dillon to the ore smelter in Encampment.

The literature already assembled at the small museum

Elevated outhouse built on a log crib in Dillon, Wyoming. The outhouse collapsed about 1960.

revealed a number of interesting characters, and offered an explanation or two concerning the two-story outhouses.

Ed Haggarty found the blue rock in 1897 while herding sheep on the high slopes. He knew that blue meant copper, and copper meant money. His sheepherding days were over. He took a partner named Ferris and developed the deposit. Later, two others bought into the operation. The town that grew nearby was named Rudefeha from two letters from each man's name, Ferris and Haggarty bringing up the rear.

When the four mine owners barred saloons from the town that blossomed around the copper mine, the drinking faction, which comprised the major faction, moved one mile south and established their own town. They named it Dillon, after the leading saloon man, Malachi Dillon. It was a strange town — no one ever called it ordinary. At its peak it had several dozen log homes and eight buildings on Main Street, six of them saloons. Malachi's had a sign over the bar, "FREE MEALS IF YOU DRINK ENOUGH."

The buildings along Main Street were fronted with boardwalks elevated above the road, built "high as a mare's back." No one ever shoveled snow off the streets — they just tramped the snow down under foot and hoped that it never came above the boardwalks. The heavy snows also brought about the ultimate refinement of one of man's most basic necessities, the outhouse. In Dillon, the elevated outhouse, and indeed the two-story outhouse came into its own.

Old-timers claim the outhouse began its spurt to new heights when a father of four got fed up with shoveling the path to the outhouse. It seems the thundermugs were filled from the previous night, and the emergency call was being sounded by two of the young ones. Dad was clearing the path through two feet of snow in a valiant race with the call of nature. For the third time that month, Poppa lost the race and suffered the abuses of an irate spouse faced with another foul mess. With the conviction of a man driven by anger, but possessed of a solution, the father went straight to the local carpenter and gave explicit instructions:

"Build me another outhouse, and put the damned thing on top of the snowbank! If we get another heavy snow, I'll have you build another one."

No one knows how many he had built, but he most definitely started a new architectural trend in Dillon.

By the next fall, nearly everyone had elevated his outhouse and had built "summer steps." Some built log cribs three or four feet high and placed their outhouses on top. Most dug pits and built outhouses on enclosed stilts, but those few who relied on the crib as the waste receptacle got a surprise the night of the first hard freeze. As the residue froze and expanded, the cribs split open with a resounding *crack!* These structures remained solid until spring, when severe listing made their use hazardous.

Many folk built new outhouses that matched heights with the second stories of their homes. The sanitary house was reached simply by going upstairs and walking out the connecting "gangplank." Some outhouses were twenty feet tall. There was no use made of the "lower floor" on most of these structures. The free-fall distance was nearly twelve feet. On a quiet day there was little privacy.

A few outhouses reportedly utilized both floors. A full-length dividing partition separated the two. Given the choice, an old hand would prefer to use the upper floor. It was quieter and drier, though more aromatic.

Back in Encampment, the local madam solved the snow problem a different way. She built an enclosed walkway to the privy to eliminate snow shoveling and to ensure the privacy of her customers. Business boomed.

In 1901, young newsman Grant Jones, already saddled with a severe drinking problem, but possessed of a magic pen, started a newspaper called *The Dillon Doublejack*. The first issue carried the following:

Courtesy Encampment Museum

Remains of a two-story outhouse that was once connected to the second floor of the largest hotel in Dillon, Wyoming. The rooflike structure at mid-height is actually the collapsed portion of a catwalk that gave access to the hotel's second floor. Both levels of the outhouse functioned. Note the single outhouse on a log crib to the right.

To the most distinctive brotherhood in the world, the boys of the drill and the pan, whose members see the word welcome on fewer doormats, and know more about hospitality, travel over more miles of land, and see fewer railroad tracks, eat more bacon and see fewer hogs, drink more milk, condensed, and see fewer cows, worship nature more and see fewer churches, regard women with more chivalry and see fewer of them, judge men better, and wear fewer starched shirts, undergo more hardships and make fewer complaints, meet more disappointments and retain more hopes than any class of men in the whole wide world — to the brotherhood of quartz and placer prospectors and miners — I dedicate the DILLON DOUBLEJACK!

Jones, who apparently never bought a meal since his drinking always qualified him for the free eats, had a grand way with words. His wild stories of rare animals which he called his Alco-Colic stories, were published in many nationally circulated dailies. Half the country read of his Cooly Woo, that could dig itself to safety in solid rock, and the Bockaboar that had short legs on one side for traversing slopes at high speed, but often got dizzy from rotating ever clockwise. There was also the One-Eyed Screaming Emu that could disappear by swallowing itself in one huge gulp.

Editor Jones had a great future, but he died suddenly, just six months after his arrival. It seems that he drank himself into a mild fit, and when he began to see strange creatures, his pals administered a "shot" of morphine. Morphine was available over the counter then, but dosages were a bit vague. He died, they say, from "an advanced case of sociability, complicated by good intentions." He became one of the first to disprove his own oft-made statement: "In Dillon there are no morgues, no graveyards, and no dead ones."

Courtesy Encampment Museum

Grant Jones, the short-lived, hard-drinking editor of the *Dillon Doublejack*.

The reconstructed two-story outhouse built on the museum grounds in Encampment, about twenty miles east of its original location at Dillon, Wyoming.

Encampment

I VISITED ENCAMPMENT a number of times, checking the progress of the museum and the reconstruction of the two-story outhouse. Eventually both reached completion. On those occasions when weather permitted, I would travel on up the "road" to Dillon, past the old deserted towns of Rambler, Copperton and Battle. Placed almost equidistant from these towns, a bronze plaque claims that while fishing in the area, Thomas Edison got the idea of using a carbon filament in his as yet unsuccessful light bulb.

I searched Dillon several times. Nothing in the way of outhouses remained worthy of a photograph, but one mile north, the remains of the Ferris-Haggarty Mine were quite spectacular. The main structure still stood astraddle the shaft. At its foundation flowed a small stream, tumbling over the same blue rock that signaled Haggarty's original discovery.

Haggarty and his partner did well by selling the operation for $1 million in 1902. In 1908, the price of copper dropped and the operation ceased. Five thousand people left the area. Now you would have trouble rounding up five folk in the deserted towns sprinkled about the mine.

Encampment survived and became a quaint village in the foothills, populated by ranchers, a few storekeepers, and nature lovers escaping the city. Part of its charm is its slow acceptance of the niceties of modern civilization. Each time I entered Encampment, I was taken by the sign in front of the gas station: "Indoor Toilet." It seemed to strike the proper note.

The remains of the Ferris-Haggarty Mine just north of Dillon, Wyoming. The small stream at the base of the building flows over chunks of copper ore, bringing out its bright blue color.

Part of the Ferris-Haggarty to Encampment tramway, the longest in the world at the time of its construction.

Things are quiet now in Encampment, Wyoming.

On my last visit to Encampment I was directed to the tiny cabin of an old duffer who had returned recently from a visit to an old folks' home nearby. Jim lived a frugal life, mainly with the help of friends and neighbors. He filled in

All the modern conveniences. Notice *S* added to explain a later improvement.

many of the missing details, and added a new chapter to the art of growing old.

Jim was leading a happy life, living in his little cabin, sponging a bit here, making a buck there, when well-meaning folk decided he belonged in the old folks' home a few miles north. They left Jim no choice — he was packed up and moved "for his own good." Jim found his new home quite unsatisfactory, but he had a plan to rectify the situation. He invested his last dollars in six quarts of whiskey and got the entire population of the home roaring drunk. They kicked him out, and he returned to his little cabin, broke, hung over and happy.

Horse Shoe Springs

WORD GOT AROUND the college, the town, and eventually the state, that some strange character at the college was looking for two-story outhouses and other odd structures, which many residents interpreted to mean *hog ranches*. Hog ranch, it seemed, was a term given to any house of ill fame — whorehouse, that is — located near a military installation.

As to why they were called hog ranches, there were several explanations. One suggests that such an establishment was operated by a man named Hogg. Another suggests that since many of these houses specialized in good food, as well as close company, perhaps the name came from the offering of pork on the menu. Most likely, the name came from the physical make-up of the usual crib ladies.

Whatever the background of the term, my curiosity was again piqued, and I decided to include a few hog ranches in my next tour of the area, along with forts, an old mining town or two, and any other sights that might have an outstanding outhouse or unusual story.

I stopped at Horse Shoe Springs a few miles south of Glendo, Wyoming, mainly because it was on my route. It was once the home of Bad Man Slade, who at the age of thirteen began his evil career by killing a man with a rock. His father promptly sent him West from his home in Illinois, but he continued with the killing habit, finally reaching the lower end of a taut rope in Montana.

The site of the old stage station is presently occupied by the Lancaster Ranch. The owners showed me around, proudly

At the Three Mile Hog Ranch, each crib, or small room, had its own door. Inside there was room for bed and walkway. Calamity Jane is documented as having been one of the gals at Three Mile.

pointing out the bullet-proof, triple-walled structure of the ranch house that replaced the stage station. They told me of the Indian fight there in 1868. Frequently referred to as the Bloody Trail Massacre, it is one of the best documented fights involving Chief Crazy Horse. It was also one of the very few times that Indians attacked at night and in midwinter.

Captain Smith and four troopers were at the old station when sixty-seven Indians, led by Chief Crazy Horse, accosted them. The Indians soon retired behind a butte four hundred yards away. Two scouts sent out by the captain were promptly chased back. Portholes were opened, the door barred, and the fight was on. Two Indians were killed.

In midmorning, two other troopers, chased by Indians, managed to break through and arrive at the station. It was now seven against sixty-five.

The men in the station had nothing to drink but Red Jacket Bitters, which did much for morale, but little to improve accuracy with a rifle. Two men were sent out to get water, but quickly returned with a report that the Indians had gathered at the well.

At 10:00 P.M., the Indians set fire to the building, forcing the troopers to crawl through the twelve-foot tunnel that led to a sod dugout, filling in the tunnel behind them. The station burned, and while the Indians celebrated, the men dug out and escaped with their belongings, including a ten-gallon keg of whiskey.

The Indians found the troopers the next morning a few miles south, on the trail to Fort Laramie. One trooper took an arrow in the eye, but promptly yanked it out, eye and all, and went on fighting. Another soldier was hit above the eye, loosening a flap he had to hold up with one hand. He was killed as the group ran for better cover. Another trooper was killed and mutilated. The troopers were now down to five men, three of them wounded. One badly wounded man had to be left behind as the group took new positions. He committed suicide. It was now four troopers against forty Indians.

With only nineteen rounds of ammunition left, the troopers called for talks. Chief Crazy Horse, who spoke English, was willing, and promptly commended the men for their valiant fight.

"You four very brave — we kill only three of you." This prompted an attempt to barter whiskey for lives, and both sides agreed to walk back to the whiskey cache.

The whiskey was turned over, with the tap open and the suggestion that the Indians take it back to their camp and drink it there. There was no stopping the Indians. They set to drinking right where they were, and the troopers took off down a ravine. A few shots were fired at them, but pursuit was forgone lest a turn at the keg be lost. The four troopers eventually got to Fort Laramie and safety. They had lost all their belongings, but others had lost more.

Fort Laramie, like most of the forts in the West, had no stockade. This fact contributed to the fort's most embarrassing moment during the summer of 1864.

For three days a large detachment had been scouting the area for Indians, splitting into small groups to search for sign. They met back at the fort, unsaddled, and adjourned to the barracks while the horses rolled on the parade ground. Thirty Indians suddenly materialized and chased off the horses! It took an hour for a hundred soldiers to begin their fruitless pursuit. The Indians, constantly changing horses, had little trouble outdistancing the troopers, who were stuck with one horse apiece.

Fort Laramie

TODAY, much of the Fort has been refurbished to show the way it was. One can almost see the soldiers on parade, the cheers and horseplay on payday, or imagine Jim Bridger outside the Sutlers Store smashing lice in the seams of his clothing, using two flat rocks, while regaling off-duty soldiers with tall stories.

John Hunton, a prominent hay rancher in the late 1800s, was a friend to many of the famous men and women that visited the Fort Laramie area. Men like Hi Kelly, Bat Garnier, Heck Reel, Wild Bill Hickok, Portugee Phillips, Jim Bridger, Slippery Sam Slaymaker, Calamity Jane, and the famous stage driver, Thomas C. Todd, champion drinker who claimed, "I ain't drunk 'til I'm flat on my back pukin' straight up!"

Hunton's diary, released some years after his demise, carried a number of fascinating entries. One concerned the solution to a forty-dollar robbery:

> Tom Wilson's money recovered from Pat Corbliss after hanging him a little. Nice Day.

As to Calamity Jane:

> Her achievements have been very greatly magnified by every writer I have read, for she was among the commonest of her class. She seldom ever carried a rifle when riding horseback from place to place, and I do not think I ever saw her with both rifle and pistol. Her one redeeming trait was that she seldom spoke of what she had done or could do with gun and pistol. . . . I first saw her in about 1875. My ranch was a gen-

Old wood building next to the grout crib house at Three Mile was probably the saloon that attracted the soldiers from the dry grounds of Fort Laramie.

eral road ranch and place of entertainment for the traveling public . . . Jane often stopped at my place, especially 1876, 77, 78. She worked often at hog ranches at Fort Fetterman and Fort Laramie until General Crook's army organized in May 76 — when she and three other women of same character were smuggled out with the command and remained with it until found out and ordered back.

Later in his diary, Hunton states that Calamity Jane worked as one of the girls at a house of ill fame, and that "she wasn't one of the better ones."

And about another famous character whose name Hunton spelled his own way:

I will now refer to J. T. "Wild Bill" Hicock, [*sic*] whom I knew fairly well in 1874 and late in the year 1875. . . . During that time I do not think he knew "Calamity Jane" or had ever seen her. . . . In less than a month I heard of Bill's death. He was assassinated at Deadwood by a stage driver, Jack Mc-Caul, who was lynched for the deed, by a mob reputedly led by Calamity Jane, but at that time Calamity was in the hands of the Military authorities (Crooks Army).

As to John Hunton's expertise at judging women, he left no question that he had plenty of experience. For many years before his demise, he lived with a woman and kept it secret from his wife. He had no hesitation to tell all about the second woman in his diary.

Wyoming had two famous hog ranches, one on the Bozeman Road just north of Fort Fetterman near Douglas. The other, called Three Mile, was three miles west of Fort Laramie on the Cheyenne-Deadwood Stage Road. Since liquor and loose women were barred from the military forts, these houses had to exist outside the three-mile radius of prohibition imposed by the army.

The girls were referred to as painted ladies, fallen angels, sportin' women, crib women, tenderloin ladies, and generally were the lowest of the lot. The food and booze were good, and change was often given in brass tokens good for a few "skull benders" at the bar, or for service in one of the small rooms or cribs.

The association of "red light" with houses of ill fame reportedly came from the railroad men's habit of leaving their lanterns outside the door. That term was seldom used around the hog ranches, since the nearest railroad was seventy-five miles south.

Three Mile is now a respectable ranch. When I first visited the site, the new owner had just discovered the questionable history of his acquisition. He had recently torn up the floor boards of the saloon and crib areas in the old grout building that made up the original hog ranch. He found a few coins, some tokens, and evidence that someone had gone over the same ground earlier. It seems that at least two people figured that change tends to fall out of pockets easily when the clothing deviates from the vertical.

Kirwin

THE MAN ON the telephone was positive, and the fact that he had made a toll call lent considerable credence to his story.

"I have found a perfect two-story outhouse for you, and it's only sixty miles away."

I left immediately, stopping by his office in Douglas, Wyoming, to obtain directions. He seemed a bit less sure of himself after our discussion revealed that his find had only one door.

Half an hour later, and fifteen miles south, I located the structure, which turned out to be unusual in that it was indeed very tall, perhaps fifteen feet. A single door opened to a roomy seven-by-seven foot space, only partially occupied by the necessary facilities. The upper portion was composed of slatted vents, making this the sweetest smelling privy it had been my privilege to visit. Those living nearby explained that the building was once the air vent for a large underground potato storage area. One gentleman was sorry that I had not found an honest two-story privy, and suggested I look into the old deserted town of Kirwin, across the state, where he personally had seen the real thing.

Kirwin was another false lead, but as always, something interesting happened on the way to the site.

A sign at the turnoff to a ranch a few miles from the town site read:

NO HUNTING
NO FISHING
NO NOTHING
DON'T ASK

Hot lead on a two-story outhouse cooled rapidly when the tall, but single-floor outhouse was found to have been made from an old potato vent.

I drove in and asked. The rancher got a kick out of my asking
— said he had met a lot of fine but stubborn people because
of that sign.

On an earlier trip, I had noted a sign of a different nature
that was even more effective:

Hunters, Fisherman And
Trespassers Welcome
$200 Per Day Trespass Fee
Pay At Hdqtrs. 2 mi East.

The welcome sign wasn't out at Kirwin either. First there
was a locked gate on a public road, which upon close inspec-
tion revealed a big padlock on a heavy chain, but with one
open link hidden behind the gatepost. A sneaky way to discourage travel on the road, even though it led to a forest service campground, as well as the deserted town site of Kirwin.
I entered and drove ahead only to be stopped by a man with a
gun. I asked entrance — he denied same, explaining he was
hired by a mining company. I claimed public road, he
chuckled. I got out a six-pack of beer. He put away the gun.
Half an hour later, I drove on up to Kirwin, waving back at
my new friend who made me promise to stop by on the way
out.

Forty miles west of Meeteetse in west central Wyoming,
Kirwin sits in a narrow valley, 9200 feet above sea level, surrounded by steep slopes leading to the high peaks of the Ab-
sarokas. It was beautiful — almost like a bit of Switzerland.
Old mining equipment, long idle, lay scattered about, covered with a deep layer of red dust, no longer capable of prob-
ing the earth for copper and molybdenum.

Mine shafts penetrated the ground in a dozen places. A
barrel-type hoist bucket rested on the ground next to the
Wolf Mine. A large building nearby had to have been a
boardinghouse. Upstream on the north bank of the tumbling
stream stood the tall remains of the Tumlum (or Tumalum)
Mine. It seemed to be just the right situation for a tall privy

The Wolf Mine at Kirwin, Wyoming, has been out of use for nearly one hundred years. Note the coarse slab siding, and the wooden rain gutter.

Tumlum or Tumalum Mine had its gallows wheel structure enclosed — a tribute to the severe winters in the area.

or two — high altitude, steep slopes, and most likely subject to heavy winter snow accumulations. There were no doubt a few tall ones in town at one time, but none remained — not even short ones.

In 1935, long after the mines had shut down, Amelia Earhart filed claim on a beautiful high bench above the Tum(a)lum Mine. She ordered a cabin built shortly before one of her long transoceanic flights. Work on the cabin was suspended when word arrived that Amelia was missing over the Pacific.

Walls three logs high, a door jamb, and a small wooden airplane on a pole with its propeller spinning in the wind, stand as a small tribute.

Construction on Amelia Earhart's cabin was stopped abruptly when word of her disappearance arrived. Note the propeller windvane, a small tribute to her profession.

Bonneville

BONNEVILLE, and a number of other small nearly deserted towns lay on my route home. None of the settlements had sewer systems, and were prime prospects for tall privies.

A sign on the main highway points north to Bonneville. It's an official highway sign, two feet by four feet, and big enough for one to believe that indeed town can be reached via the gravel road that lies adjacent. I had driven north a scant three miles when I was confronted with an old-fashioned ford. It was perhaps two hundred feet to the far side where the road took up again and became the main street of Bonneville. In the center of the broad sandy expanse was a small creek, perhaps an inch or two deep and twenty feet across.

I was about to drive across when I noticed several faces pressed to the window of the railroad station across the creek. When two fellows ran outside the building to watch, I chickened out and walked over to the railroad bridge and picked my way across the ties.

The men were crewmen for the Burlington Northern Railroad, waiting for the train to arrive in order to relieve the crew on board. I came along just in time to offer a bit of entertainment.

The ford, I was told, was pure quicksand. They explained that it was used only in the winter when the creek was frozen. The alternate route to town from the highway to the west was used at all other times.

According to one of the crew, several old cars lie deep within the quicksand. One case, he said, was spectacular.

The quicksand ford leading to Bonneville, Wyoming.

Some years ago, in early spring, the driver of a late model car got a run for it and almost made it across. He was stuck up to the running boards but was able to scramble to solid ground and hike to the nearest "big" town for help. A few hours later, after the car had sunk to the roof, a caterpillar tractor rumbled up, and a cable was dug down to the windows. The cat pulled and pulled, and finally the car slowly responded — but only the body of the car came free, leaving the frame and wheels to join the ever-growing crop of relics deep beneath treacherous Bad Water Creek.

In 1919, a trestle upstream washed out and spilled a freight train into the creek. Half the train threatened to sink out of sight. It took weeks to rebuild the trestle and recover

Courtesy J. T. Border
Caboose in the clutches of the quicksand of Bad Water Creek.

Typical residence in Bonneville is built of old ties and trestle timbers.

the engine and some of the cars. The caboose and parts of some flat cars washed downstream to sink into the quicksand.

But the most spectacular event to hit Bonneville was the big explosion that blasted the little town in 1921. A truck driver, delivering 750 quarts of nitroglycerin to the Birdseye Mine, hit a ditch and — KA-BLOOOEEE! — blew a hole in the ground big enough to bury a house. The biggest piece left of the truck was the armature from the generator. Most of the houses of the town were built stoutly of used ties spiked together, and consequently weathered the blast with only a loss of window panes. Those houses still stand, some occupied as vacation homes.

The windows in town blew out a second time when a miner walked into the local bar with a stick of dynamite jammed in his hip pocket. A two-foot fuse extended from one end of the red stick of explosive. Someone lit it!

Lost Cabin

L OST CABIN was a few miles east. There might be a tall outhouse, or at least a tall story there. It was the latter — a tall story — but true, of course.

Lost Cabin, like Bonneville, is located on Bad Water Creek, and the only store in town, Okie's Store, sits in the middle of town. According to Mary Helen Hendry, a local Wyoming historian, a gang of bullies blew into town one day, and one of them promptly proceeded to intimidate store proprietor, Okie. The roughie pulled a gun, shot into the ceiling and shouted, "I'm a bad man from Stinking Creek." Fast thinking Okie snatched up a rifle and replied, "Well, I'm the stinking man from Bad Water Creek," and backed the bad man out at gun point.

Dale City

SOME WEEKS LATER I set out for Dale City, Wyoming, where reliable information led me to believe a two-story outhouse made out of rock used to stand. Dale City sounded like a good bet, since all the structures in town were said to be built of rock. Outhouses and jails are both strong and tend to outlast larger buildings. My chances looked good!

The jail stood, but the outhouse either never existed, or had been dismantled in order to improve some other structure. But as usual, a memorable story emerged to fill the void.

A few miles to the northeast, the Union Pacific, in 1938, built a trestle across a deep ravine. Indeed, the construction of Dale City was a result of the work crew's extended residence while constructing the 200-foot-high, 650-foot-long masterpiece. It was the tallest and largest on the Union Pacific, but it was doomed to cause trouble. No allowance had been made for the gale force winds that plague that part of the country, particularly at the change of seasons.

Soon the trestle joints loosened, making passage dangerous. A dozen long guy wires designed to eliminate the sway were bolted to the tracks, extending to deeply embedded anchors. In one season, the wires were stretched, and the sway was back. The crews of freight trains were so frightened of the trestle, that they made it a practice to stop short, pile out, and flip a coin to see who walked across alone. Then the engineer would set the throttle on dead slow, and the crew would watch the train cross the trestle a cappella. After

A two-story outhouse? Right in the middle of the deserted town of Rock Creek?

the train was caught and stopped, the rest of the crew would walk across and resume the trip. Crews of passenger trains had to gut it out in order to foster passenger confidence.

On the way home from that trip, I took a back road, hoping to stumble across a truly unusual outhouse. As if I had willed it, a tall structure appeared ahead next to an old deserted house. It was twenty feet tall, had a door below and a door on top, accessed by a built-in ladder. My heart leaped and I grabbed for the cameras. I shot two rolls of film of the exterior, then opened the lower door. The room was empty except for a big rusty pipe running from floor to ceiling. The floor was covered with sawdust, several feet deep in the corners.

The upper door opened to reveal a large insulated metal tank. The pieces began to fit together. This was an elevated water supply and ice house combination. Water in the top and ice below offered ice cold water on tap all summer long.

What a comedown. In all my travels about the state, I

No, it's not an outhouse — it's a combination water tower-ice house.

had found remains of just one tall privy, the one in Dillon. Although reconstruction of the privy was under way, the fact was I had searched most of my home state and photographed not one two-story outhouse.

It was time to branch out. Perhaps Montana would be more productive.

Part II – Montana

Jardine

OCCASIONALLY THE OBVIOUS seems to elude a person, especially when he gets deeply involved in a subject — sort of like not seeing the trees for the forest.

It finally became evident to me that tall outhouses were to be found at northern latitudes or high altitudes. The mountain state of Montana should therefore be a prime source for two-story outhouses.

I knew there were tall outhouses of a sort in Virginia City, Montana. I had photographed a few of them some years before, and had taken somewhat suspicious note of the reconstructed tall outhouses in nearby Nevada City.

Both towns deserved a second look, and this time I would not be distracted by the usual sights — old mines, saloons, dredges, and the like.

I laid out a tour of Montana starting just north of Yellowstone Park at the old mining town of Jardine; working west to Virginia City; then north, following the Rocky Mountains; then east; then north again to the Little Rockies near the Canadian border. As leads developed, I could plan a zig-zag return to Wyoming. It looked like a three week trip of about three thousand miles.

I packed sleeping bag, cookstove, food and cameras. I figured on camping out a lot, staying at a motel every four or five days to maintain a taste for civilization, and developing a few rolls of film as proof of my camera's integrity.

Jardine was a quiet place when I visited it a few years before, but now the town was almost as busy as it had been during the mining days. The nearby slopes were being groomed as ski runs, construction of several lifts was under way, and new cabins and lodges were sprouting up all over the place. The suspiciously tall thin structures viewed on an earlier trip seemed to have vanished. There would be no second look. The old outhouse behind the mill was still intact, and was still only one story high. It was, however, an outstanding structure, well engineered for its purpose. It looked from the outside to be about one outhouse deep and four wide. The inside was bare except for two long poles. You could walk the length of the outhouse on the narrow floor, and take your ease anywhere on the lower of the two horizontal poles, then lean your back against the upper pole — sort of a two-point suspension, mid-thigh and mid-back. No doubt it was designed for minimal comfort to discourage loafers. The logs were well polished by the hundreds of mill workers who labored at the site from 1917 to 1948.

Jardine might have been a disappointment, but an incident that occurred on the road to Virginia City brought my sense of humor back to normal.

It was a long straight stretch of highway, and far ahead I noticed a man walking along the center line. As I drove closer, I could see he was staggering. His stagger worsened as I coasted toward him. I came to a stop as he spun around a full 360 degrees and collapsed dead in the middle of the blacktop. I had a strong urge to hop out and lend a hand, but something looked fishy. His collapse was too perfect — just like the kind John Wayne did as a green actor, and kids everywhere imitated for the next twenty years.

I held my place behind the wheel and studied the man. His clothes were tattered and dirty. His face was tanned and creased with wrinkles. He looked like a circus clown without makeup. As I watched, an eyelid flickered, and in the instant, I could see his eye was trained on me quite precisely. That did it — I backed up and drove around him, pulling off to the side of the road a few hundred yards beyond.

The noise of an approaching car brought about a most

Tall structure photographed in Jardine about 1969 was not investigated at the time. In 1984 it was gone. Note the wood crib on top of the log crib.

spectacular recovery. The bum was instantly on his feet, wobbling along the center line, cocking a careful but fleeting eye on the approaching car, letting the stagger increase to another full turn, ending with complete collapse on the center line.

This man was quite an actor, and it turned out, a talented panhandler. When offered assistance, he would slowly recover, stagger a bit, refuse a ride, but put the bite on for a bit of the green stuff.

I watched him operate for nearly an hour. He batted a bit over 500, netting folding money from each successful ploy, and recovering instantly from each failure.

When he noticed that I was watching, he put on an even better show. He was up to a three-turn dying spiral, going for an Oscar when I finally left the scene.

One of several deserted mills in Jardine. It is visited by horses more often than by humans.

Virginia City

VIRGINIA CITY was much the same as I had remembered it; quite commercialized, but thoroughly fascinating and essentially genuine. Although most of the buildings in town were burned as firewood in the post-boom years, a rich core of buildings remains on the dozen or so square blocks that make up the business district of this town that once claimed more than ten thousand citizens.

The site would have remained pristine prairie had not Bill Fairweather and six friends camped at the head of the gulch a few hundred yards to the south. When Bill unlimbered his gold pan and washed a load of gravel, he uncovered the richest placer deposit in the world, and started a gold rush that would eventually move $100 million in gold from the ground into the miners' pockets. The discovery was in 1863, and within a year the gulch was named "Alder," and a town called Virginia City exploded into existence at a rate of almost one hundred buildings per week!

Nevada City and Bannack

IN 1864 MONTANA TERRITORY was established, with Bannack declared as its capital. One year later, Virginia City took over as capital by virtue of its overwhelming population, only to lose it to Helena in 1875.

The boom years of 1863 to 1868 brought about some strange incidents involving the towns of Virginia City, its suburb to the west called Nevada City, and its rival, Bannack, just eighty miles west. The road connecting these towns became the playground for a bunch of dry land pirates who held up, robbed, plundered and murdered. From June to December of 1863, the gang robbed and killed more than 190 men. When a particularly brutal and bloody murder was committed just prior to Christmas, the citizens rose up in anger and organized a vigilante committee of five hundred. Within six weeks, twenty men had been hanged. Frank Parish, George Lane, Haze Lyons, Jack Gallagher, Boon Helm, and Club-Foot George Lane stretched vigilante ropes from the exposed beams of a half-finished building in Virginia City. A club-footed man should have known he would be recognized, mask or no mask. If this begins to sound like a silent movie plot, then hang tight — it gets better.

The sheriff of Bannack, elected in spite of his recent prison record at San Quentin, offered to cooperate fully with the vigilantes. But on the sly, he met with his cronies and planned the very robberies the vigilantes were sworn to stop. The gang held secret meetings over the livery in Virginia City, in the roadhouse later to be called "Robbers' Roost," just west of Nevada City, and of course in the sheriff's office in Bannack. The sheriff, it seems, robbed the public at night and chased after himself during the day.

The double life of Sheriff Henry Plummer was revealed when a robbery victim spotted scars on the back of one of the robber's hands. Foolishly, the robber-sheriff had removed his glove in order to unlock a strong box. The alert observer later saw those same scars on a hand attached to Sheriff Plummer. They hanged Plummer and his two deputies in Bannack.

Two other suspected gang members, Captain Jack Slade and John "the Hat" Dolan, were hanged at Nevada City. Slade was notorious as the winner of a number of "fair fights," one of which involved shooting with a gun hidden under his coat. Slade was apprehended for being drunk and disorderly, and apparently hanged as a public service. Both Slade and Dolan asked for clemency, their excuse being that they were drunk at the time of the crime. Some folk in the crowd suggested that they each be given a few drinks so they could be hanged drunk, all in the interests of justice.

The Chinese moved into Virginia City when the original placer miners moved out. At one time, six "companies" of Chinese, about six hundred men, worked the diggings near town. A serious rift came about over boundary lines, and the six companies split into two factions. The argument escalated to fights and then to an all-out war. They fought for two days and shot up all their ammunition without killing a soul on either side.

When they resorted to hand-to-hand fighting with pick and shovel, two men were fatally injured. Eleven Chinese were tried for the killings. All were released for lack of positive identification. White witnesses claimed all the Chinese looked alike. Chinese witnesses, with great wisdom, agreed!

Filled with a strong sense of history, I drove to the Cornucopia Mine overlooking Virginia City. From there I could glass the buildings in town. I spotted the old brewery, the saloon, the livery, and Sauerbuer's Smithy, where oxen were slinged and trussed for shoeing. And back there, behind the

Chinese store and other places of business are fronted by well-worn boardwalks. They were formerly lit by old gas lamps. Now they've converted to electricity in the town of Virginia City, Montana.

dry goods store, and also behind the old Richard Cook residence, were two tall outhouses!

Behind Hanna and Mary McGovern's Dry Goods (toys a specialty) was a single-seat outhouse rising more than fifteen feet in the air. Its floor was seven feet above ground level, the loftiness of the structure made necessary by the downward slope of the ground at the rear of the store. A

Elevated outhouse behind the dry goods store has lost contact with the store's rear entrance. Note the second outhouse to the left for ground level use.

small deck led from the store's rear entrance to the door of the outhouse — almost an inside outhouse.

The Richard Cook residence was built on ground that was comparatively level. The outhouse that looked tall from afar was actually floored a modest four feet above ground — hardly worthy of a photograph.

I sauntered about town, enjoying authentic items, ignoring the commercial. Finally I entered the Bale of Hay Saloon and had a drink for old times' sake, then stepped outside and put the spurs to my trusty steed. (I had a coke and climbed into my pickup.)

Nevada City was just a mile and a half to the west of Virginia City. I had to stop and see how the reconstructed two-story outhouse had fared.

The first time I visited the site, I was amazed to see that the outhouse was not a working, functioning relief station, although it certainly looked like it was usable. It had fooled a number of tourists. Instead of being built with a free-fall chute from upper seat to the pit below, it simply had an enclosed bench with a cut out seat. And of course the tourists used it. After one season it was full.

The second time I visited the site, they had placed a pot under the seat. Of course, the pot would have to be emptied frequently.

This was my third visit, and this time the upper door was boarded shut. There is a lesson there somewhere, having to do with reconstructing faithfully or not reconstructing at all.

Most of the items in Nevada City were either moved in or recently built, not so much as an historical effort, but more as a matter of free enterprise. The old hotel in Nevada City was originally the Salisbury Stage Station, once located near Ruby, Montana. It is worth a look, but it would have been better if it had stayed in Ruby.

Fifteen miles west of Nevada City on the south side of a road set back in a cozy grove of trees, is the marvelous old roadhouse once called "Daley's Place." Pete Daly (Daley)

Reconstructed nonfunctional two-story outhouse in Nevada City, Montana, has been a problem to hotel owners. Visitors insist on using it.

built it and ran the establishment as a stopping place for travelers on the Virginia City – Bannack road. For several months he offered bed and meals plus entertainment. Rooms on the first floor were labeled "Bachus [sic] and Lady Luck" (dining and gambling), and the second floor was termed the "Terpsichore — Ardent Swains and Seductive Sirens," (entertainment areas).

Within six months the roadhouse became one of the se-

Nevada City Hotel was once the Salisbury Stage station of Ruby, Montana.

cret hideouts for the Plummer gang, and that stretch of road east and west became the bloodiest, most dangerous eighty miles in the territory. Later, Pete Daley's Tavern became known as the Robbers' Roost mentioned earlier.

If you look closely you will see the symbol **3-7-77** scratched in the logs of the building. Perhaps it was a code or a password, but like Zorro's **Z,** it always showed up after the vigilantes caught up with and dispatched an outlaw or two. That same symbol appeared in other towns at other times, perhaps as a warning to local crooks that the vigilantes were watching.

The town of Bannack is now a state park and a national

Robbers Roost, originally Pete Daly's roadhouse, became the hangout for outlaws working the Virginia City to Bannack road.

historic landmark. Among the buildings now preserved are two old jails, the Masonic hall built in 1874, a school that dates from 1871, and a classic frame church constructed in 1879. But the crowning glory is the beautiful brick building known as the Meade Hotel. Built with class, and intended to last, it sported

The Meade Hotel in Bannack, Montana, had high ceilings and spiral staircases.

two stories, each with eighteen-foot ceilings, a spiral staircase six feet wide, double-decker porticos and vaulted windows at the front.

At the south edge of town, a five-ton mill was still in operation. "Five-ton" means it can crush five tons of ore each hour. They were extracting concentrated ores of silver, lead and zinc, with a few traces of gold. The mill is a bit of an antique, but it runs and pays a profit. It's a frugal operation, and no money has been wasted on paint. Off to the side are two outhouses, and in keeping with the operator's economic policy, only one has a sign on it, and that sign reads, "WIMMIN."

Gold was found on nearby Grasshopper Creek in 1862, one year before the Virginia City strike. Bannack's boom was less spectacular, but longer lasting than its rival to the east. It grew to a population of one thousand by 1863, and spurted to more than three thousand a few years later when the hand dug ditches brought badly needed water to the local placers.

Any diligent ghost town buff is bound to note that the last buildings to collapse and disappear are the jails and outhouses, no doubt because they are both strong. Although the latter may be strong in more than one sense, it remains a fact that the shorter the dimensions, the stouter the structure.

Bannack has two jails, both over one hundred years old. One, the smallest and oldest, has two tiny barred windows. The larger jail has a guard room and two cells. One cell is dark, the other has a three by three-foot picture window barred with straightened wagon wheel rims bolted to the logs. The nuts are on the inside, but much to a prisoner's disappointment, the bolts are peened over. The doors are doubly layered and three inches thick.

When Sheriff Plummer and his two crooked deputies, Buck Stinson and Ned Ray, were finally cornered by a vigilante group of five hundred, they faced the possibility of spending some time in their own jail. History is a bit unclear at this point, but it is probable that the three crooks were spared the night in jail and were hustled immediately to the gallows at the

Built in 1862, Bannack's first jail offered maximum security and minimum ventilation.

edge of town. When the sheriff's turn arrived, he begged for his life, but finally settled for one last request. "Give me a good drop," said Sheriff Henry Plummer, and the vigilantes obliged. And the number **3-7-77** mysteriously appeared on several buildings in town.

Bannack's second jail had bars made from straightened wagon wheel rims.

Broadwater

COLONEL CHARLES A. BROADWATER made his first fortune in Bannack in 1862. Later, he invested in other profitable ventures, including mines, stocks and short line railroads.

The colonel had a dream, and in 1888 he had more than the $500 thousand it would take to make that dream a fact. He envisioned a large sprawling two-story hotel, a big covered pool, trolley cars, and a placid lake with boats floating serenely about. It would be a spa the size of a small city, and people from all over the country, perhaps the world, would vacation at Broadwater, and the town of Helena a short mile east.

His business advisers told him that the population in the area could not possibly support the endeavor. It would be a loser unless the colonel could bring a railroad into Helena, Montana. That should be easy, the colonel figured, for he was a railroad man.

The complex was finished in 1899, complete with a two-story, two-block long hotel with two tall turrets, and hundreds of rooms. The entire length was fronted with second-story balconies. The trim was oak, and the carpets were velvet plush.

The natatorium was 100 feet by 300 feet, with circular windows and a Moorish exterior, accessed through a vaulted doorway bracketed by two tall towers, each one topped with a thirty-foot lightning rod. Inside, two waterfalls tumbled over rocky precipices, one offering pure cold water, the other, warm mineral water. Steam radiators lined the sides, and

Broadwater, Montana, was big and beautiful and was intended to attract the elite from around the world.

potted plants gave it a tropical atmosphere. Johnny Weismuller learned to swim in that pool, and his later fame would add to Broadwater's name.

The colonel saw his dream completed, right down to the lake, the boats, and even the trolley. He died at the age of fifty-two of influenza, three years after "America's most famous health resort" was completed. The railroad was yet to be built.

Perhaps the fates were kind to the colonel, for the spa called Broadwater was to suffer many ills in the years that followed.

Floods wiped out the lake, the boats, and the trolley in 1925, and an earthquake caused severe damage to the hotel and plunge in 1935. The plunge was torn down in 1946.

The undamaged portion of the hotel served as a gambling casino for a time. Then, after lying vacant for a number of years, it was auctioned off piece by piece, a window here, a cupola there, and an entire porch somewhere else. Remnants of its majesty now can be found sprinkled about the country as conversation pieces, playground structures, or front lawn gazebos.

Only the rock waterfalls remain from the natatorium at Broadwater, where Johnny Weismuller learned to swim.

Ringling

THE MUSEUM at Helena, Montana was rich with information concerning old towns and deserted mining camps. The museum staff helped me make a list of those places that might have heavy snowfall and be candidates for two-story outhouses. An old-timer overheard our conversation and volunteered that I should check on Castle and Ashland. I added them to my list and revised the balance of my tour of the state.

My loop to the north of Helena was fruitless. I did, however, stumble upon an interesting example of the local humor.

A new highway was under construction that would make a straight line where the old road took an S curve around a two-hundred-foot-high rocky promontory. The new grade aimed straight for the middle of the promontory. Obviously a deep cut would be required. Some wag, no doubt with mountain climbing experience, had painted a broad dashed line from ground to top, then laboriously printed alongside, "CUT ON DOTTED LINE."

I stopped to photograph the scene, but found the light was wrong. My plan to take a shot on the way back was somehow foiled. I have often kicked myself for not camping on the spot and taking a photo in morning light.

The route to Castle in west central Montana took me through the nearly deserted town of Ringling. The name itself was enough to cause me to stop and inquire, but the two marvelous old churches had me scrambling for the cameras. Of the dozen or so ramshackle buildings in town, only two showed any sign of life — the post office and the bar. The door to the bar was fully screened, but was six inches too short, leaving a wide gap at the top. I studied the mismatch of door and frame as I entered. The bartender looked up and said, "Keeps the dogs and cats out."

I was his only customer, which made conversation easy. He knew a lot about the town and told me where to find old-timers who could fill in any gaps.

Originally the town had been called Dorsey. When the town moved a few miles to intercept the Milwaukee Railroad,

One of the many deserted residences that stand in Ringling, Montana, once the home of the famous Ringling Circus folk.

Catholic church in Ringling, Montana, now offers shelter for a resident flock of pigeons.

it was called New Dorsey. In 1900, when Mr. Ringling, of circus fame, bought ninety thousand acres nearby and hinted that he might make the town his headquarters, the town folk fell in line and renamed the place Ringling. The population in town and the immediate vicinity at that time topped one thousand souls, many of them homesteaders from Iowa.

Apparently no one realized that a circus was on the road all summer, and would most logically make their winter quarters in some warm place like Sarasota, Florida. The circus did set up at the edge of town, most likely as a sort of dress rehearsal to get ready for the summer tour. That happened twice, and each time the town grew a bit, expecting something permanent. There was the Ringling Market, with a sixty-foot ramp to the second floor dance hall, a cement jail, a huge community hall, and two grand churches.

When the circus folk moved out, the town slowly died. Two fires in the thirties wiped out most of the homes. Now the old decrepit bar is the bright spot in town. The sign behind the bar seems eminently appropriate "RECOMMENDED BY DRUNKEN HEINZ."

The bank was torn down in 1969 because the owner "just felt like it," and was tired of paying taxes on an empty building.

When the town forgot to pay county taxes on the community hall, some "strangers" sneaked in, bought the hall for back taxes, and tried to take over the town. No one objected.

The old Catholic church has lost most of its shingles, right down to bare roofing boards in some places. The two chapels at the front are still used, but the main portion of the church, minus its windows, has became a spacious home for the resident flock of pigeons.

The Congregational church served as a school for a while, but for the past twenty years it has been unused and untended.

Castle

THE BARTENDER at Ringling knew little about the town of Castle, further up the mountain, but he did point me toward an old-timer named Berg in another small town along the way. It was time to leave — a second customer had wandered in and the place was getting crowded.

Oswald Berg, of Lennepe, Montana, was born in 1891 in the town of Castle. He was two years old when the town folded, but, it has been his hobby to gather information on the now deserted town. When asked about a two-story outhouse, he lit up and leaned forward to tell me about it. It was attached to the Castle Hotel, and had a catwalk from the second floor to the upper floor of the outhouse.

Oswald told of seeing the old hotel register, and being taken with the large flowery signatures and the fact that everyone registered for each night in residence. He implied that the outhouses were seldom used. The patrons preferred chamber pots, known affectionately as "thundermugs," in their bedrooms. The rooms were heated, and the outhouses were not.

Apologetically, Oswald told me that the outhouse was gone, and probably the hotel with it.

I drove on up to Castle, hoping that Oswald might be mistaken about the outhouse. He wasn't. But the town itself still held an impressive number of old buildings, including an old brothel or two, recognizable by the small cribs made by dividing ordinary upstairs bedrooms.

The town had a rather boring history, with only a few high spots to hold the reader's interest. The first silver and lead claims were filed in 1884, the most promising being the Cumberland. The town that sprang up was named for the rocky outcrops that stood like castle towers above the treeline.

By 1898 the town reached a population of two thousand. There were five thousand in the area. Shelby Dillard published *The Whole Truth,* a newspaper in which he exaggerated the value of the claims, the profits of the mines, and the ebullient quality of the citizenry.

Only a portion of the many buildings that fronted Main Street in Castle, Montana, have survived the hostile winters.

It was a high-class town, although it had seven brothels, which were never called by their baser names.

The Cumberland Mine Company, tired of spending profits hauling ore to Helena, built their own smelter, only to find that it cost almost as much to haul charcoal in as it did to haul ore out.

The Jawbone Railroad (it took a lot of talking to get it

A few remnants of the Cumberland Mine, biggest producer in Castle, Montana.

built) reached the outskirts of town in 1891, but frequently suspended operations in the winter because of heavy drifts over the tracks.

A smelter exploded in 1892, and a year later the town collapsed when the silver market fell after the repeal of the Sherman Act.

The population dwindled rapidly, but editor Dillard, apparently believing all the great claims he had printed, hung on until his readership deserted him.

Finally, only two men remained in town. One winter, with heavy snow limiting their travels, they found themselves short of food. One of them managed to walk off the mountain, returning a few days later laden with food, but in a state of exhaustion. His friend welcomed the groceries and offered him a cup of coffee. Soon the exhausted man left for his own cabin, a short distance away. He died before reaching it, and the population of the town was now one. A newspaper in the area ran the headline, "Half of the Population of Castle Dies in Snowstorm."

Zortman, Landusky and Ashland

THE LITTLE Rocky Mountains of north central Montana spawned three mining towns in the 1880s and 1890s. Zortman is presently the most active, with about fifty souls, one bar, a cafe, an old jail, and a church. "What more would you want," remarked the bartender. Under slight urg-

An overview of Zortman, Montana, business district, with saloon at right and salvation on the hill.

ing, he continued with the recent highlights of life in Zortman.

"A few years ago," the barman related, "one of the heavier drinkers fell asleep in an old Essex parked outside. His buddies painted all the windows black, and the poor guy slept three days."

With a bit of a sidelong glance, he continued, "Why just last winter when I was tossing out the late drinkers, fixing on closing up for the night, in comes a bunch of guys lugging a forty-foot pine tree. Couldn't hardly close up with that thing sticking out the door — had to stay open all night."

Zortman's jail has seen better times — but they still keep the door padlocked!

The Ruby Mine stretches over a considerable distance. Waste material was simply dumped in the ravine.

The late drinkers formed a tight group. In some ways they reminded me of Charlie Russell's statement about drinkin' buddies:

> If you want to know a man, get him drunk and he'll tip his hand. If I like a man when I'm sober, I kin hardly keep from kissing him when I'm drunk. This goes both ways. If I don't like a man when I'm sober, I don't want him in the same town when I'm drunk.

Just west of Zortman a few miles, are the considerable remains of the old Ruby Gulch Mine and town. More than $25 million in gold was taken out of the mine, and old Swede, the caretaker, and also one of the men who painted the windows of

Extensive trestle made a level connection between mine adit and mill at Ruby Gulch, Montana.

the Essex black, claims that he took $4 million out by himself, but lost it all in the bar.

A massive trestle was required to reach the rich vein that outcropped high on a steep slope. The trestle curves in to the mill and smelter, then becomes a road that is, in turn, the main street of the small town.

The mine shut down in 1942 and the school closed its doors in 1949, but all the seats, the blackboards, even the coat hooks await the next class.

Just outside of town on a sharp curve to the right, there is a sign reading, "50 FOOT DROP TO THE LEFT — NO CUSHION." It looked like some of Swede's handiwork.

Landusky, a dozen miles or so southwest of Zortman, was a hell-raising sort of a town. It was the home of miners who illegally mined gold in the nearby Indian reservation.

Powell "Pike" Landusky, for whom the town was named, arrived in the area in the 1880s in the company of two hard cases on the run. Pike was immediately involved in a brawl with ordinarily friendly Indians. After shooting a squaw "by accident," he suffered a gunshot wound to the body and one to the jaw, removing four teeth and part of the jawbone. The recovery was slow and painful, causing a lifetime rage to set in, and finally causing his death a dozen years later.

The four Curry brothers came to the Little Rockies sometime later as homesteaders, and it wasn't long before Pike had trouble with them. Pike returned a borrowed plow in a broken condition, claiming it was fractured before he borrowed it. Bad

Ore cars are still lined up at the entrance to the Ruby Mine at Ruby Gulch, Montana.

feelings developed, and later, when the Curry boys were suspected of rustling, Pike, now a deputy sheriff, volunteered to escort them in chains to the nearest judge. On the way, he took the opportunity to get even by beating the boys rather badly.

The boys were found innocent and returned with vengeance in mind. The Curry brother with the baby-face, now called "Kid Curry," and possessing the hottest temper, led his gang to Jake Harris' Saloon in Landusky, looking to have it out with Pike.

Pike was tipping a drink when the Kid slammed him on the back, then planted a fist on Pike's bad jaw when he turned. The Kid proceeded to beat Pike to a pulp, while his brothers held the audience at gunpoint. Tiring, the Kid stepped back, and Pike, flat on the floor, drew his forty-five. It misfired. Kid Curry shot him dead.

The Kid skipped the country and joined up with Butch Cassidy and the Sundance Kid. They claim that the Kid came back in 1966. Some say he wanted to visit old friends. Others claim he had money stashed nearby. That same rumor about Butch and Sundance as well as Kid Curry, is voiced in a dozen old towns throughout the western states.

A dozen old-timers had told me of a genuine two-story outhouse in Ashland, Montana. One of them even had a postcard picture as proof. Ashland, in southeastern Montana, was on my way home. I was saving the frosting for last.

It was gone! Torn down just a few years before! My disappointment was tempered, however, for there was a marvelous old solid brick outhouse just a block away. It was a small version of the palatial two story brick house that stood in front. Both had fancy cornices, inlaid cross brick patterns, and identical roofs. I had often heard of a brick outhouse but in somewhat baser terms. I studied it, and indeed, it certainly was built. It was time to head for home.

The old frames the not so old in Landusky, Montana.

This old chair, made with loving care and often repaired, rocks gently in the wind on a porch in Landusky.

The Good Old Days (Minnesota)

THE DIFFERENCE between an antique and a piece of junk is often a matter of judgement, and our judgement depends upon our age and the age of the item in question. Let those miserable heaps of broken equipment — tractors, combines, furniture and cars — reach an age of fifty or so, and we consider them valuable.

It seems that each generation looks back to an earlier time for reminders of a pleasant past. It's a human trait, I guess, to remember the best and forget the rest. The OLD days, properly aged, become the GOOD OLD days.

Perhaps that explains my interest in outhouses. In my early years I helped my father build an outhouse behind a cabin on a small lake in northern Minnesota.

Dad was a particular sort and finicky about the design and placement of what he called the "path." He referred to our homemade cabin as a "wilderness home with five rooms and a path."

The little house had to match the construction of the cabin, right down to the miniature hip roof and log slabs that laced through each other at the corners, like the intertwining fingers of a man in deep contemplation.

The outhouse had to open to the East, and had to be placed so that the door would not face the cabin. The door had to swing in, which seriously limited the space inside, but Dad had his reasons. The lane from cabin to outhouse was nearly straight, with gentle curves to add class. Trees were planted on either side of the door to create a "fetching entrance."

Inside, we built a multi-sided stool instead of a simple plank seat, and on the stool we placed a genuine toilet seat and lid. A vent connected the stool assembly to the outside through an enclosed chute that led to the roof. A sack of lime took up residence in the corner, with a long-handled dipper hanging nearby ready to neutralize each deposit. Two small screened windows high on opposite walls provided cross ventilation. The shape of those vents was the topic of family discussion. Moons? Stars? Perhaps an owl cut out to go along with the family name of Weis, pronounced 'Wise.' I have forgotten just what shape was finally used, since the discussion dwindled when the difficulty of cutting intricate patterns in the log siding became evident.

It's not likely that my father ever read the little eighteen-page booklet written by Chic Sales entitled, "The Specialist." This charming little essay, in bound form, sold over a million copies in dozens of countries. It detailed the thoughts of a man who specialized in building outhouses. Although he makes no mention of the two-story variety, he does present some very good ideas, most of which my father incorporated in his masterpiece as a matter of common sense.

For example, the East facing door let one view the sunrise during the morning's constitutional, — and that's where the inward opening door was essential. One could hold the door open with a foot, but quickly shut the door and hold it shut, should another customer arrive. It would be awkward with an out-swinging door. A person could find himself exposed while leaning out the door, feeling for the handle.

The straight path was a matter of efficiency, especially for nocturnal use. As Chic put it, "that ain't no time to be stumbling around on some winding path."

There were five youngsters in our family, and I was right in the middle, agewise, a spot reserved for the family idea man, often referred to as the black sheep or the hell-raiser. One of my milder ideas was to photograph family members going to the outhouse, with a movie camera set on slow speed, then catching their exit on high speed setting. When projected, this showed everyone running to the outhouse and sauntering back, which sort of proved Chic's idea concerning the straightness of the path. We could have had a curved return path, and it would have been a great idea to run that path past the woodpile, so two jobs could be done on one trip.

"The Specialist," I learned many years later, had suggested this ploy, even to placing the woodpile beside the outhouse, claiming that a hired girl would bring in ten loads of kindling in one day — more if she was the shy sort. It helped to put a return spring on the door so that the outhouse always appeared to be occupied.

The only thing my father neglected that "The Specialist" recommended, was to "paint her two color and contrasty, since dark ain't no time to be scouting around."

We always carried flashlights at night, but that was primarily to avoid skunks which abounded in the area, especially late in the summer, when garbage pits attracted the little varmints from miles around.

One morning my younger sister, Jessica, returned from a quick visit to the little house out back in a rather agitated state. She claimed there were "funny noises out there."

My brothers and I offered comfort and explanations. "Now you've got to figure on funny noises in outhouses, Jess. It's one of the little entertainments provided by nature." Jess huffed and gave us an imitation of the mysterious sound that was between a cough and a snort. "That's normal," we told her, and explained that it could be even louder if she altered her diet. When Jess got down to foot-stomping, we figured she was serious, and decided maybe we should have a look.

Jess was right, for down in the pit, standing on a small mountain surrounded by a moat, was a very disconsolate skunk sneezing on the lime that covered his head and back, making that strange sound just like Jess had imitated.

We could see we had a problem that needed discussing. After long debate, we decided to shoot the skunk and make a

quick getaway in case of gas attack. I took careful aim while
holding the lid up with one hand and the door open with a
foot. Jess stood in the doorway with the lime sack. I shot, Jess
dumped the lime and ran out the door. I dropped the lid,
slammed the door and ran for cover.

There wasn't a bit of stink. Word of my success spread
along cabin row, and my services were sought out. I dispatched dozens of skunks from garbage pits and crawl
spaces. My fame spread throughout the county. I considered
it a public service since some of the skunks were suspected of
being rabid.

When a store owner in the nearby town of Park Rapids
asked me to take care of a skunk trapped in his window well, I
quickly accepted the challenge, proud to demonstrate my tal-
ents. I promised the owner an odorless solution.

I asked for a shovel, dug a hole out in the alley in which to
bury the skunk, then placed the shovel handy in the window
well. My client was impressed. I took careful aim at the spot
that experience had shown would result in an instantaneous,
no smell demise. A careful squeeze, and bang! The job was
done, except that the "dead" skunk's tail slowly rose, and he
sprayed and sprayed and stunk and stunk! The proprietor gave
me a dirty look that plainly reduced me to amateur status. I
buried the skunk, and left the shovel too, buried to the handle,
hoping my reputation might recover as the smell wore out and
his customers returned. The smell was gone in two weeks. My
reputation was gone forever.

An uncle of mine used to brag of tipping ten crappers over
during one Halloween night. My uncle, and most other folk,
liked to use the term "crapper," but I always considered it a
word with a blue tinge, unacceptable in polite conversation.
Such is not really the case.

Sir Thomas Crapper was the inventor of a revolutionary
valve that permitted a permanently installed bedpot to allow its
holdings to be washed down a sewer pipe. His valve involved a
trap, or S curve in the bowl to prevent odors from backing up

the pipe, and another valve to shut the flow of flush water, and permit a refill of an overhead tank. These toilets were called "Crappers," and it was as nice a word as "Van Dyke," meaning a beard.

But "crapper" had a naughty ring to it, and soon other variations of the word became common. It's one of those rare words that got smutty with use. Most words take on a milder everyday application with the passage of time. A word that would curl your hair forty years ago is now commonly on the tongue of the young and innocent.

When the crapper came into common use, many older homes and hotels retrofitted their facilities. Usually an upstairs room was selected, and part of the floor elevated to allow room for the plumbing to be placed under the stool. This was much easier than tearing up the ceiling of the room below. That platform gave rise to the term "throne," and the room became the "throne room," a noble place to situate a crapper.

Part III – Colorado

Pearl

SOME OF MY BEST tips on two story outhouses came from skiers. It made sense. Where there was heavy snow, there should also be tall back houses. Several friends had suggested I visit Crested Butte, Colorado, insisting that a number of unusual outhouses were still in use in the town proper. The nearby ski resort was quite modern, but the retired coal miners still living in Crested Butte still held on to their old values, outhouses included, according to my helpful friends.

I had high hopes of success as I drove south into the neighboring state of Colorado. My map study of the state indicated a number of possibilities. Caribou, at an elevation of 9,905 feet, must certainly have had enough snow to spawn a double-decker. Crested Butte had to be investigated, as did Lake City, where a strange case of cannibalism had occurred. And there were other towns with lesser reputations worth a look, like Pearl, Colorado, just across the Wyoming border.

Luckily, one resident remained in the little "ghost town" of Pearl, the daughter of one of the earliest settlers, by the name of Nina Rhea. Nina wasn't given to exaggeration, being more inclined to tell it the way it was. Her father, Cooke, was the leading hunting guide in the area spanning the times that Pearl grew and died. He was always suspicious of the mining that was supposedly done near town, considering it mostly fake and blue-sky. Money changed pockets, but not much ore was being moved.

Nina told of a fancy steam engine that was hauled to one of the mines by a sixteen-horse team, and how stock in the

Pearl, Colorado, a town that grew on speculation, then like a faulty firecracker, fizzled out rather than boomed.

place rose abruptly. "But the engine never turned a wheel," said Nina. "Pearl was a boom-town that never even popped."

Supposedly copper, silver and gold were mined from the Zirkle and Wolverine Mines, and indeed, in 1900, prospects looked so good that a town of five hundred folk sprang up. There were two saloons, three hotels, and forty or so homes, but no tall outhouses.

The names of various creeks and mountains in the area carried the humorous stamp of old Cooke Rhea. When a government cartographer asked Cooke the name of a certain

One of the mines near Pearl. It was mostly stock sales and promotion rather than sweat and pay dirt.

creek, he replied, "Damfino," and so it was "Damfino Creek" officially. Whiskey Mountain was the name he gave to a nearby peak for its abundance of empty booze bottles left by a wealthy English hunter. And a creek of indefinite source became "Conundrum Creek," a name certain to puzzle the greenhorn.

Caribou

T HE ROAD TO CARIBOU was steep, and three miles short of town the wind began to blow. By the time I reached 9,900 feet, the breeze had become a gale. The vehicle rocked and the trees whipped like grain. The old wooden buildings of town had taken on a list, and any tree with guts

Only the stoutest structures can withstand the high winds in Caribou, Colorado.

Caribou Mine was the richest of the half-dozen profitable silver mines that took $20 million in precious metal from the ground.

enough to grow in the open had a built-in lean. Rock wall remains of the old hotels were still vertical, but badly blasted by windborne sand and gravel. If any two-story outhouses had ever existed, they would have long since been battered and probably blown away.

It was a hostile place, and no one in his right mind would live there, unless, that is, he had a heavy interest in a mine that pumped out ore rich in silver.

Sam Conger found the outcrop in 1869. With a partner named Martin, he explored the vein, and turned up ore that quickly attracted three thousand people to the little town. They named it Caribou, for the big game (probably elk) that could be harvested nearby.

Heavy snows with the high winds caused such a hazard

Snows were deep in Caribou. Roomers in the two rock hotels of Caribou often had to enter and leave by way of second-floor windows. Note late July snowbanks in distance.

that school was held only in spring, summer, and fall. There was a three-month winter vacation. Twenty-five foot drifts were common. Miners returning from a short visit down the hill sometimes had to probe for their cabins with long cane poles. Hotel residents entered and exited through second floor windows.

In the summer there was lightning. Vicious bolts that slammed into the town seeking the heavy iron deposits that rested just beneath the surface.

But it was a moral town. In 1881, the whores and gamblers were voted out of town, and Cardinal, the next town down the mountain, inherited them.

Two bad fires removed the upper stories of the hotels and many of the wooden structures of Caribou. Epidemics of diphtheria and scarlet fever decimated the populations. The last resident died in 1944.

Crested Butte

TWO HUNDRED MILES west of Caribou, at an altitude of 8,885 feet, lie the town and adjacent ski area of Crested Butte. It is a place of contrasts.

In town, retired coalminers live on minimal funds, while

One of our first astronauts built this summer home below the ski slopes of Crested Butte, Colorado. Note the resemblance to a reentry vehicle.

This two-story outhouse, connected to the Masonic hall in Crested Butte, Colorado, was the first such structure to be found functional and still in regular use.

at the foot of the slopes, ski buffs dine on gourmet food. Lear jets wheel overhead, while old-timers tread the boardwalks. Tired skiers loll in hot tubs at the resort, but in town most homes lack sewer systems. Below the ski slopes, an astronaut has built a fancy cabin with all the conveniences, while in town, a two-story outhouse is still in use at the Masonic hall.

After I had a good look at the Masonic hall masterpiece, I wandered leisurely about town, looking for other examples of early plumbing. The town hall, a beautiful structure from the front, had a two-story outhouse attached to the back. Nearby, an old two-story saloon with twelve-foot ceilings, had a most unusual three-way outhouse accessible from the upper floor, main floor, and ground level.

Numerous houses had covered walkways leading from warm kitchens to cold outhouses — far enough to prevent a mix of odors, yet freely accessed in spite of heavy snows.

Eight or nine feet of snow on the level was common in Crested Butte, and one record year it exceeded twenty feet. Avalanches were common on the slopes above town, one wiping out the boarding house, superintendent's house, and two

Enclosed walkways, sometimes extending one hundred feet to outhouses, were common in Crested Butte.

City Hall had classy architecture at the front and . . .

At the rear of the City Hall we find a two-story "inside outhouse."

sheds of an active coal mine. Several died, but one man rode the avalanche all the way down unharmed.

The Elk Mountain House, an early way station, had the ultimate outhouse. It is no longer standing, but the memory of the building is fresh in the minds of the long-term residents. Each of the three floors had walkways leading to outhouses that dropped into a common pit. The seat of the upper outhouse was sixteen feet above ground level, and the pit was twelve feet deep for a clear (and no doubt noisy) drop of twenty-eight feet! Each outhouse also had storage space for stove wood, so that customers could do two jobs at once. The designer must have read "The Specialist" by Chic Sales.

The many covered walkways from house to outhouse fascinated me. I found one that seemed to be deserted. There was no paint on the house, the curtains were tattered, and the lawn untended. I entered an open doorway at the house end of the walkway and sauntered the dim length of the tunnel-like outhouse access. The outhouse was surprisingly clean, and still had a partial roll of paper standing by the seat. I returned to the house, considered trying the door, then decided in favor of photographing the exterior.

On the third exposure, a shadow fell over the lens. I looked up, then looked up quite a bit higher to see a giant of a man glaring down at me with great hostility. He said "Yah?" and walked into me, bumping me back while I racked my memory for a Swedish word or two. I tried *"Manya tussen tuck,"* which is Norsky for *thanks much*. He stopped, apparently unwilling to take advantage of a foreigner. I left quickly, thankful that I hadn't tried the back door of the house I had foolishly assumed deserted.

The town was presently being invaded by large numbers of free-living young people. They might be called late generation hippies. The town folk were split badly over this incursion. The young folk were moving into old buildings, occupying old mines, and were a general nuisance to most merchants, except those who found they could make a buck off the newcomers.

Signs proclaiming "No Shoes, No Shirts, No Service" were everywhere. And so were the dogs. It seemed that every newcomer had at least two dogs. One old-timer, when asked his opinion of hippies, said simply, "Dogs, dirt, and dope!"

The town was polarized and the marshall could not please both groups. When criticized, he quit. One of the town's two newspapers complained of the new leash law; the other claimed the ten dollar dog tags should be priced higher. One irate woman said she would give any dog coming into her backyard a dose of buckshot and another to the dog's owner, given the chance. A local rancher claimed he was shooting two dogs a day to protect the stock.

Crested Butte didn't deserve such controversy. It had always been a quiet place tucked away in the mountains, existing only to serve the mining industry. Originally it was a gold camp. Soon a smelter was built, and coal deposits were found nearby to fuel the smelter. The gold petered out, but the coal seams were thick, and soon the gold camp became a coal town. By 1880 there were 250 people in town, and two years later, the Colorado Fuel and Iron Company took over the mining operation, developing three anthracite and three bituminous mines.

A huge blast in the Jokerville Mine shaft killed fifty-eight miners in 1884, shortly after new "safety ventilators" had been installed. The Jokerville closed down, but remaining mines continued to serve the Fuel and Iron Company and the Denver and Rio Grande Railway until 1952, when the railroad switched to diesel-powered locomotives.

The population dropped abruptly; many coalminers retired on the spot. The town began to look like a ghost town — old, unpainted, ramshackle.

But then the ski craze hit Colorado, and Crested Butte was one of the first sites selected by developers. The new business was welcome, and the town began to perk up and clean up. Then the long-haired element arrived, and threw Crested Butte into a controversy that only time will heal.

It's still a fascinating place to visit. The mix of lifestyles is

A three-way outhouse, attached to a little used saloon and dance hall, offered inside access from both floors, and outside ground level access to the addendum.

intriguing. Old gentlemen prop their feet up against potbellied stoves, while nearby, long-haired young folk speak of the advantages of singing to one's self and the therapy of "hollering under your breath."

Second look at Masonic hall masterpiece shows upper level of the bi-level outhouse can be reached by covered stair.

I stopped by for one last visit to the two-story outhouse behind the Masonic hall. It looked like it was built by a committee, with roof lines at odd angles, and a second floor reached by way of a covered stairway or a catwalk from the upper floor of the lodge. I took photos from all angles, finding that no single view could reveal its true function.

In the upper portion of the two-story outhouse there was a sign, ANYTHING OVER EIGHT POUNDS MUST BE LOWERED BY ROPE.

Flushed with success, I set out for a site that held little promise of tall outhouses, but promised a unique tale.

A last look at the Masonic hall two-story outhouse in Crested Butte, Colorado. That's the one with a sign posted at the upper floor: ANYTHING OVER EIGHT POUNDS MUST BE LOWERED BY ROPE.

Lake City

L AKE CITY, in southwestern Colorado, lies in a high
valley a few miles north of the Slumgullion Mud Slide.
It's a modest town of several hundred year-round residents.
Each summer it booms with trout fishermen and each winter
with snowmobilers. The town grew out from a few gold and
silver mines in 1874, but one year earlier, an event occurred
that put Lake City on the map even before it existed.

Alfred Packer was serving a sentence in a Salt Lake City
jail on a charge of counterfeiting. He had voiced his knowledge of prospecting, and offered his services as guide to a
number of visitors. Word got around, and soon five men
pooled a kitty and bailed him out with the understanding
that Packer would guide them into the Ouray area. It would
cost the five men their lives, but they would become famous
in the process.

Israel Swan, George Noon, Frank Miller, James
Humphreys, and Wilson Bell, led by Alfred Packer, wandered through what is now southwestern Colorado, looking
for gold. In January, they visited Chief Ouray, a friendly
Ute, who advised them not to head east. Snow was deep, and
traveling would be treacherous, but their intrepid guide
Packer was sure they could make it.

In April, Packer showed up at an Indian agency seventy-
five miles away. He told of losing contact with his charges in
a blizzard, and nearly starving to death in the process of finding his way back to civilization. He bought drinks with money from several wallets.

Packer looked suspicously well-fed for a man who claim-

Near the Slumgullion mud slide south of Lake City, Colorado, lie the graves of five men said to be cannibalized by one Alfred E. Packer.

THIS TABLET ERECTED
IN MEMORY OF
ISRAEL SWAN
GEORGE NOON
FRANK MILLER
JAMES HUMPHREYS
WILSON BELL
WHO WERE MURDERED ON THIS SPOT
EARLY IN THE YEAR 1874
WHILE PIONEERING
THE MINERAL RESOURCES
OF THE SAN JUAN COUNTRY

Marker at grave site lists those claimed to be the edible victims of Alfred E. Packer.

ed to have been short on food. The Indians were distrustful and backtracked his trail. They found strips of flesh beside his tracks — flesh that bore little resemblance to wild game. Shortly, prospectors reported finding the bodies of five men with fractured skulls and great quantities of flesh stripped from their bones. A search was mounted, but Packer had left the country.

· Nine years later, Packer was apprehended in Wyoming. He had lived quite a normal life — even served on the bench in Montana for a time. He was hustled to Lake City for trial. Lake City by this time had become a bustling town of almost five thousand, and all five thousand were anxious to see justice done to Colorado's only cannibal.

Packer was tried for cannibalism and murder. He was found guilty and sentenced to hang by the neck until dead. The judge's exact words are lost in the legend that grew about the case, but they were no doubt similar to the many renditions, some poetic, that have survived. A poem by Stella Pavich states that the judge claimed "There were seven democrats in the county, and you, you voracious son-of-a-bitch, you ate five of them!"

Packer claimed that Wilson Bell had killed the others after they had all lost their way and run out of food. He had no choice, he explained, and when Bell tried to kill and eat him, he only reacted in self-defense. This argument brought him a new trial. He was found innocent and released, to become a recluse until his death in 1907.

Just south of Lake City, near Slumgullion Slide, at an elevation of 11,400 feet, there is a fenced-in gravesite, and a plaque commemorating the event.

At the University of Colorado, Boulder, students voted on a new name for the grill in their Memorial Union building. With great humor, and by a large majority, they elected to call it the, "ALFRED E. PACKER GRILL."

Of course, the sign over the door, either by mistake or by design, spells Packer's first name, "Alferd," thus piling more confusion on a story already overloaded with discrepancies.

The students showed their opinion of the chow at the Memorial Union grill at the
University of Colorado by voting in an appropriate name.

Part IV – Wyoming

Lost Springs

THE ROUTE to the Black Hills passed close to several old Wyoming towns I had always wanted to visit. None of them held great stories, but each had some small claim to fame.

Lost Springs, about seventy miles east of Casper, has been nearly deserted for dozens of years. The population varies between two and seven. The country store still operates, catering to ranch folk in the area. The brick bank that occupied one corner of the only intersection in town has become famous throughout the state. People would drive miles out of their way to be served through the teller's window and observe the vault being used for liquor storage — sort of a secure back bar.

The deserted gym, at what is now called the Town Hall, was a classic. The ceilings were just slightly higher than the rims on the bang boards, and hanging lights limited the clearance even more. The lights were of the pressurized gas and mantle variety, similar to Coleman lanterns. Basketballers at Lost Springs were noted for their line drive shots, and the strange dodge to the side before shooting, in order to clear the chandeliers. An old story told of another small town basketball player not so far away would be appropriate to Lost Springs, since they played outside whenever possible, to take advantage of higher "ceilings." After winning a tournament in a fancy big city gym, the ace player of the team was being interviewed and was asked how he explained his phenomenal percentage of shots from beyond the free throw circle. He replied, "Well, heck, there ain't no wind in here."

About thirty miles to the south of Lost Springs lies the long deserted company town of Sunrise, so named because the sun rose late each morning over the tall hills to the east. Like many things, sunrise seemed more precious the longer one had to wait for it.

Copper was mined here first, but the veins ran out just as deposits of high grade iron ore (hematite) were discovered. Shortly after the turn of the century, the Colorado Fuel and Iron Corporation was taking 600 thousand tons per year out of the open pit mines. The iron ore, and the coal mined at

Surface works of the Sunrise Mine in Sunrise, Wyoming, make up only a part of the equipment needed for subsidence mining.

The longest garage in the world claims to hold sixty-five cars, but has only forty-odd doors.

Crested Butte, were mated in Pueblo, Colorado, to produce structural steel.

In 1941, open pit mining was suspended in favor of subsidence mining, where the lode is removed at the bottom and the overburden permitted to collapse downward.

Recently, mining was suspended and most of the residents moved to other towns to take other jobs. As a company policy, many of the buildings have been burned to eliminate liability problems and tax assessments.

That means the long sixty-five car garage will soon go. More than five hundred feet long — so long it has to bend to match the curve of the road fronting it — it is truly one building, under one long, leaky roof. Ripley called it the longest garage in the world. Even more unusual is its location in Wyoming, one of the least populated states in the Union.

Just north of Newcastle, at the eastern border of Wyoming, the remains of a large, long-deserted coal town are sprinkled along a narrow carbon-stained valley. It was named Cambria and it was quite a going concern. But now there is hardly enough left to make a picture.

I wanted to visit the town and its suburb just west on the high flats, for an odd reason. The suburb was called Antelope City, and they had a baseball team named the "Neversweats." I had always thought that gamesmanship was a recent innovation, but the name "Neversweats" indicated that the coalminers of 1900 knew all about it. With a name like "Neversweats," the opposition is intimidated even before the game starts — and even if you lose, you lost without working up a sweat. Think what you could have done HAD you worked up a sweat!

Part V – South Dakota

Black Hills Area

DETAILED MAPS of the Black Hills area revealed a number of small towns worth looking into. Some were well known, like Keystone and Rockford, others seemed to be unknown even to the natives.

Cascade Springs is a most unusual place. Only ten miles south of Hot Springs on what was once a main highway, it now stands completely deserted. Four buildings still remain on what was once the main thoroughfare. On the north side, a beautiful old three-story rock hotel stands surrounded by tall brush. On the south side of the road, all in a row, are the two-story stone bank, the brick Wells Fargo Office, and a ramshackle old wooden building leaning against a prop. And built on to the back of that building is a *bowling alley!* A bowling alley in a ghost town! Perhaps I have lived too long!

The town dates from 1888, when a promoter named Allen heard that a railroad was to pass by his favorite spring. He gathered investors and built a small version of the hot springs spas to the north. But alas, the railroad bypassed Cascade Springs, gracing the town of Edgemont instead.

At the extreme western edge of the Black Hills, amid dense stands of tall pines, lies a relatively modern "tarpaper" ghost town called Tinton. Traveling west from Lead, South Dakota, following a topographic map, I was surprised at the lack of any kind of road signs at the many dirt road intersections. I stopped at a cabin to check my route, and was informed that Tinton was yet a dozen miles away, and was indeed deserted, but had lately become the hangout for a full grown mountain lion.

First an old mine shack appeared, then a head frame house

Main Street of Cascade Springs, South Dakota, holds the Allen Bank, the Mercantile, and hidden under the trees, a saloon-bowling alley combination.

Bowling alley added to rear of saloon utilized small pins and grapefruit-sized balls — one of the first duck pin alleys in the area.

Bathhouse-hotel combination was built beside a small hot spring that town builder
Allen hoped would outdo the larger hot springs to the north.

clinging to a hillside above a small lake. A badly bent sign held
the logo, "Fansteele Metallurgical Co." Shortly, I passed by the
edge of town, but continued to explore the buildings beyond.
Two ball mills stood with flapping rusted metal sheeting. One
had "1945" stamped in a vertical beam. There was a sign on
another mine building, "Dakota Tin and Gold Co.," and the
number "8–1939," which I assumed meant that August, 1939
was the date of construction.

Back in town, I noticed an old deserted car of unfamiliar
contour. The name plate showed it was a DeSoto, causing me to
speculate on the date of its desertion. It probably gave up the

Tarpaper-covered shaft head building was headquarters and first stage concentrator for the Rusty Mine.

ghost some two dozen years earlier, putting the lifespan of Tinton somewhere in the vicinity of 1939 to 1950.

I followed the two-lane road, wandering through the nineteen buildings standing in good order and surprisingly intact. Most of the residences were covered with red tarpaper, but underneath they were much more substantial than mere shacks. The large community hall was of standard wood construction, but many of its windows were broken out, boarded over, or replaced with chicken wire. In one place, the wire had been breached, and I crawled through. It was one big room, with a stage at one end, with a bang board made from an old barn door hanging over. In the corner was a pile of newspapers, twigs and old clothing. It looked like a king-size mouse nest. Then I re-

View of well shaded town of Tinton, South Dakota, shows most residences to be covered with red tarpaper.

membered the warning about the mountain lion. With all deliberate haste I returned to the opening in the window. The sudden screech that accelerated my passage through the chicken wire turned out to be a metal sign blowing against a steel post!

There were tracks, however — big pug marks that I traced and later identified as those of a puma, or mountain lion.

I nosed about the remainder of the town with great care, peering into each building before entering. Nine of the residences were identical, indicating that this was probably a company town. Several more imposing homes no doubt went to the owners and bosses.

There were more pug marks around the little white schoolhouse. I settled for a photo of the exterior.

Hermosa means 'beautiful' in Spanish, and the little town at the eastern edge of the Black Hills is indeed that. At one time more than a thousand folk lived in the quiet tree-shaded town. Now there had to be a party to accumulate one hundred.

Once called the Battle River Stage Station, it later became a rough-and-tumble gambling town. During its wilder period, it is reported that a foreigner with a particularly annoying personality frequently visited the local bar. After one long evening of suffering under the man's constant bragging, the locals plotted a rebuttal.

The next morning, the pestiferous one stepped out of his boarding house and walked to the outhouse. With care, loyal residents of Hermosa estimated the time it would take the man to declothe and settle into position. Then, a lariat was thrown around the outhouse and tied to the pommel of a saddle. With a whoop, the horse took off. He was traveling full tilt when the slack took up and jerked the outhouse clean off its underpinnings, leaving one surprised foreigner caught with his pants down.

Rochford, buried deep in the middle of the Black Hills, is typical of many old towns that suddenly grew around precious metal deposits after the area was opened to the white man.

Community hall had most windows boarded over, but one window, covered with chicken wire, had been broken through, giving access to the town's only resident — a mountain lion.

Home of Anna B. Tallant, early visitor to the Black Hills and long-time teacher and postmistress.

Old jail in Rochford, South Dakota, was lined with steel plate; it was built with brick inside and rock outside.

Anna D. Tallant journeyed to the Black Hills in 1874 with a party of thirty men, when it was still illegal for whites to trespass on the sacred Indian land. They built a stockade and prospected until the army kicked them out. Anna returned in 1877

Standby mine and mill at the east edge of Rochford, is now so rotted that snooping about is hazardous, especially on the trestles and stairways.

and helped establish the little town of Rochford. She was schoolteacher and postmistress until the town faded, less than ten years later.

Although there are no fascinating outhouses, there are a number of classic buildings, making it worth a visit. The old jail, low-ceilinged and windowless, remains as originally built, lined with quarter-inch steel plate. A number of boardwalks front buildings on Main Street, some with trap doors leading to basements under the stores and shops. The Standby Mine and Mill stands by at the east edge of town, an imposing structure of uncertain strength. It gathers character as it weathers.

Myersville

A FEW MILES to the south, next to the old Alta Lodi Mine, stand the remains of the little town of Myersville, sometimes called Myers City. The town is of little note, and would not be mentioned here if I hadn't stumbled upon a fascinating old book in the attic of a deserted home. It was entitled:

EVERYBODY'S GUIDE:
or
THINGS WORTH KNOWING
by: R. Moore

and was copyrighted in New York in 1884. I spent the entire afternoon reading that book, amazed at what was known in 1884, and even more amazed at what was claimed to be fact concerning diseases that are still not understood today.

The book starts with recipes, including a dandy for a bread claimed to cure indigestion:

DYSPEPSIA BREAD. — The following recipe for making bread has proved highly salutary to persons afflicted with dyspepsia, viz: — 3 quarts unbolted wheat meal; 1 quart soft water, warm but not hot; 1 gill of fresh yeast; 1 gill molasses, or not, as may suit the taste; 1 teaspoonful of saleratus.

In the farmer's receipts chapter, this little gem to save a favorite horse:

TO CURE BROKEN LEGS. — Instead of summarily shooting the horse, in the greater number of fractures it is only necessary to partially sling the horse by means of a broad piece of sail, or other strong cloth placed under the animal's belly, furnished with 2 breechings and 2 breast girths, and by means of ropes and pulleys attached to a cross beam above, he is elevated, or lowered, as may be required. By the adoption of this plan every facility is allowed for the satisfactory treatment of fractures.

Alta Lodi mine and mill near Myersville, South Dakota.

A long deserted miner's cabin in Myersville, South Dakota.

There was much more, including a method of curing a balky horse by spinning him about, and a method of doubling the quantity of manure from a given animal!

In the medical department, we have:

RULES FOR ACTION, VERY SHORT BUT VERY SAFE. — In health and disease endeavor always to live on the sunny side. Sir James Wylie, late physician to the Emperor of Russia, remarked during long observation in the hospitals of that country, that the cases of death occurring in rooms averted from the light of the sun, were four times more numerous than the fatal cases in the rooms exposed to the direct action of the solar rays. When poison is swallowed, a good off-hand remedy is to mix salt and mustard, 1 heaped teaspoonful of each, in a glass of water and drink immediately. It is quick in its operation. Then give the whites of 2 eggs in a cup of coffee, or the eggs alone if coffee cannot be had. For acid poisons give acids. In cases of opium poisoning, give strong coffee and keep moving. For light burns or scalds, dip the part in cold water or in flour, if the skin is destroyed, cover with varnish. If you fall into the water, float on the back, with the nose and mouth projecting. For apoplexy, raise the head and body; for fainting, lay the person flat. Suck poisoned wounds, unless your mouth is sore, Enlarge the wound, or better cut out the part without delay, cauterize it with caustic, the end of a vein is cut, compress below. If choked, get upon all fours and cough. Before passing through smoke take a full breath, stoop low, then go ahead; but if you fear carbonic acid gas, walk erect and be careful. Smother a fire with blankets or carpets; water tends to spread burning oil and increase the danger. Remove dust from the eyes by dashing water into them, and avoid rubbing. Remove cinders, & with a soft, smooth wooden point. Preserve health and avoid catching cold by regular diet, healthy food and cleanliness.

CURE FOR DRUNKENNESS. — Warranted a certain Remedy. Confine the patient to his room, furnish him with his favorite liquor of discretion, diluted with ⅔ of water, as much wine, beer, coffee and tea as he desires, but containing ⅛ of spirit; all the food — the bread, meat and vegetables steeped in spirit and water. On the fifth day of this treatment he has an extreme disgust for spirit, being continually drunk. Keep up this treatment till he no longer desires to eat or drink, and the cure is certain.

CURE FOR LOCK JAW, SAID TO BE POSITIVE. — Let any one who has an attack of lock jaw take a small quantity of spirits of turpentine, warm it, and pour it on the wound — no matter where the wound is, or what its nature is — and relief will follow in less than one minute. Turpentine is also a sovereign remedy for croup. Saturate a piece of flannel with it, and place the flannel on the throat and chest — and in very severe cases three to five drops on a lump of sugar may be taken internally.

And another dandy cure for croup, although details on the
method of collecting ingredients are unstated. Obviously one
must follow the goose about with an empty tin and wait for a
propitious moment.

> CERTAIN CURE FOR CROUP. — Goose oil and urine
> equal parts. Dose 1 teaspoonful. A certain cure if taken in
> time.

Also, this about speech impediments and sleep:

> STAMMERING. — Impediments in the speech may be
> cured, where there is no malformation of the organs of artic-
> ulation, by perseverance, for three or four months, in the sim-
> ple remedy of reading aloud, with the teeth closed, for at least
> 2 hours each day.

A view down the main drag of Myersville.

Necessary Rules FOR SLEEP. — There is no fact more clearly established in the physiology of man than this, that the brain expends its energies and itself during the hours of wakefulness and that these are recuperated during sleep. If the recuperation does not equal the expenditure, the brain withers; this is insanity. . . .

And in the chapter on "Useful Hints to Grocers:"

CHEAP VINEGAR. — Mix 25 gals. of warm rain water, with 4 gals. molasses and 1 gal. yeast, and let it ferment; you will soon have the best of vinegar; keep adding these articles in these proportions as the stock is sold.

GHERKINS. — Take small cucumbers (not young) steep for a week in very strong brine; it is then poured off, heated to the boiling point and again pour on the fruit. The next day the gherkins are strained on a sieve, wiped dry, put into bottles or jars, with some spice, ginger, pepper, or cayenne, and at once covered with strong pickling vinegar.

We are also told how to make butter and place it in a tub or firkin. It occurred to me that if one stores his pickles in a butter tub, he would have a firkin of gherkins!

There was more, a great deal more, in that book. Hints on curing damp walls, keeping meat fresh by soaking in buttermilk, how to stain glass, sharpen saws, lay rock, make paint, and repair watches.

I'm a better man for having read it!

Myersville's finest home, where the 1884 book, *Things Worth Knowing,* was found in
the attic.

Part VI – Texas

Terlingua

PAT DAY used to be a good and trusted friend, right up until he gave me the champion of all bum steers.

Pat frequently drove from Midland, Texas to Casper, Wyoming as a representative of an explosives firm. On each trip, he drove past a strange old building that he felt certain was a genuine two-story outhouse. His certainty was no doubt colored by his desire to have my wife and me visit his family in their brand new home.

A few years ago, shortly after Christmas, we weakened, and set out by car for the vast wasteland called Texas. It took two days and eight hundred miles of driving to reach Dalhart, Texas, near the site of the oft-mentioned two-story outhouse.

It stood on the west side of the road, leaning slightly to the right amid a solid blanket of foot-deep snow. A small staircase led to a substandard size door. My hopes evaporated as I stooped to enter. The place was bare except for a shoulder-high rectangular opening and a sheet of one-eighth-inch-thick steel against one wall. Pat Day's two-story outhouse was an old deserted skeet house!

Of course I photographed it, figuring on using it as ammunition to tone down Patrick should he wax too eloquently in the future. He was properly embarrassed, apologetic, and full of southern hospitality during our brief stay with the Day family.

In an attempt to salvage the effort of traveling the considerable distance, we traveled on to the Big Bend country of

Texas, in search of a bit of history, and perhaps an interesting outhouse or two.

Eighty miles or so east of Presidio, near the small settlement of Lajitas, on the edge of a relatively flat plain, stand the remains of the adobe and tin town of Terlingua. Some history buffs claim that *Terlingua* means 'three forks;' others lean toward 'three languages' (English, Spanish, and probably a local Indian tongue).

Indians had long ago found a strange orange rock that turned almost red when moistened, and occasionally dripped a silvery liquid. It was considered of little value until 1884, when Juan Acosta had it assayed and found it was a very high grade mercury ore called cinnabar.

A number of small operations started up, but remained relatively unimportant until Howard E. Perry entered the pic-

The two-story outhouse that the author drove eight hundred miles to see turned out to be a deserted skeet house.

Adobe outhouse served the local school kids. Building in the background was the mansion of Howard E. Perry, prime mover of Terlingua, Texas.

ture. Perry was greatly disliked from the start. He paid workers $14.50 per week, from which he deducted $12.50 for store accounts and medical expenses.

Mercury vapor, present in huge quantities from the roasting of cinnabar, was breathed freely, causing heavy salivation and loss of teeth. Fifty years later it would be learned that it also caused serious brain damage, particularly in the young.

Perry built a company town, then rented homes, store space, and even the school to the citizens of Terlingua. Of the seventy-five adobe buildings, the store brought the best fee; the school came in second at six hundred dollars per year.

In 1906 he built a mansion in Terlingua, and lived the life of a king. King of the mercury mines which he ran with a heavy

Head frame of Mine No. 245, just east of Terlingua, is framed by doorway of miner's cabin.

hand. During the 1920s his production peaked at five thousand flasks a year at forty dollars a flask. But his kingdom evaporated in 1944 when his tax problems and bookkeeping irreg-

ularities caught up with him. He died during his trial that year,
and the various mines and buildings in town were auctioned off
at a bankruptcy sale.

Rock from which miner's cabin was constructed was more substantial than the deposit
of mercury ore in the mine nearby.

To Texans, Terlingua might look quite ordinary, but adobe schools, adobe houses, and especially adobe outhouses fascinated me. The one near the school was a classic, with double-stall sections each for boys and for girls.

Mine No. 245, a few miles east of Terlingua, held a number of old buildings with two-foot-thick rock walls and a head frame that stood over a deep, unprotected shaft. A rock, dropped from the top, bottomed in eight seconds, indicating a depth of nearly one thousand feet.

The Rio Grande wound its serpentine course a scant twenty miles to the south. It was surprisingly narrow, shallow, and easily waded. We saw no indication of massive immigration, in spite of the total lack of fences or warning signs. Two mule pack trains approached us from the Mexican side, then detoured at the sight of our cameras, giving us pause to think, and to click with care.

Over eggs ranchero the next morning, I read in the paper of Senator Proxmire's Latest Golden Fleece Award. The United States Department of Energy received dubious distinction for spending twelve hundred dollars to build a double-glazed outhouse with a southern exposure. It was designed, the department said, "to put you in the mood for meditation," and in proper "governmenteze," it was officially described as an "Above Ground Aerobic and Solar Assisted Composting Toilet." Of the 257 proposals, this was the winner!

Part VII – Arizona

Oatman

SOME YEARS AGO, I made a fool of myself in the old hotel bar in Oatman, Arizona. The place was full of signs designed to amuse the reader or to embarrass the unwary. One sign, reading "For Sale Cheap, One Henway," looked a bit fishy, so I sipped my beer and waited. Finally another outsider weakened and asked, "What's a Henway?" and the bartender replied, "about two pounds."

Feeling smug, I inquired about another sign that said "Ask about a free ring." Next to the sign was a box of "gold" rings. The bartender asked if I wanted a free ring, and I replied in the affirmative, only to have him reach over and yank a loud bell, advertising the baptism of yet another greenhorn!

On that same trip, I had noted a large photograph of a two-story outhouse, and now that such structures had become my specialty, another trip to the old town of Oatman was clearly necessary. And while I was in the area, there were some other sites in Arizona and Nevada that might prove interesting.

In 1918, Oatman had dozens of active mines, and a population near fifteen thousand. The Americana Mine became the largest producer of gold and silver, and when it shut down in 1942, disaster struck the little town. Americana tore down its mill, its hotel, the Honolulu Club, and dance hall.

Anna Eder, who owned much of the remaining town, could no longer find prospectors willing to go shares for a grubstake. Her stores went unrented, and her whorehouses were in little demand. She died penniless.

Now the town has few year-round residents, and caters

The only unusual outhouse in Oatman. The rock crib was unique.

to tourists, especially in the winter. But this is a town with a flair. One store claims it is "Open Sat and Sun 10–4 and Perchance During the Week."

A cafe advertises "Ragged Ass. Miners Steak," with the period after the "ass," making it perfectly clear that it is an association rather than a portion of the anatomy.

Wild burros enter town each afternoon. One year-round resident claimed the number of burros rivals the population

ell worn photo of a two-story outhouse that hung in the hotel at Oatman, Arizona. ne photo carried no label or information, and no one knew where the outhouse originally existed.

at times, then added, "Yup, the jackasses pert near outnumber the jackasses."

The burros are relatively tame, but occasionally nip fingers when the handouts slacken, and have been known to imperil life and limb during the not infrequent fights. Blackjack and Whitey are in a constant battle for herd leadership, and frequently scatter tourists right and left as one chases the other down Main Street and off into the hills. On one such occasion, Blackjack wandered back with a cut under one eye, and half an hour later, Whitey sneaked in from the other direction, with a chunk taken out of his rump.

The wild burros visit Oatman every afternoon for a handout of popcorn and candy.

Overview of Oatman, Arizona, showing quartz outcrop above town. Such outcrops meant mineralization, and acted as a magnet to prospectors.

The photograph of the two-story outhouse was still hanging in the old hotel. I studied it, even removed it from its frame to see whether a location had been written on the flip side. The owner of the building had no idea where the outhouse might have been built, or even where the photograph had come from. There was nothing to do but buy a sack of popcorn and feed the burros and think about traveling on.

Part VIII – Nevada

Gold Point

G OLD POINT, population eight, stands on a slight rise
   surrounded by dusty flats in south central Nevada.
Once a silver mining community, it now sees only the odd
visitor.

By the old gas station, a sign reads "Filtered Gasolene,"
and behind one residence was an outhouse that made the trip

Powder house outhouse of Gold Point, Nevada, source of a variety of stories.

worthwhile. At first it seemed to be made of concrete blocks, but on close approach, these blocks turned out to be empty explosive boxes that once held dynamite. Quite appropriate, I thought, and so did the operator of a nearby country store. He told me the old story, with new gestures, about the returning serviceman who came back to his small town with a pocketful of back pay and a few souvenirs, like a live hand grenade or two. He was determined to rid the old home of the unsightly outhouse, but failed to realize grampa was in the outhouse when he pulled the pin and dropped the grenade through the crescent-shaped ventilator. Up she went in a thousand pieces and a cloud of dust. But there, staggering out of the dust and debris, came grampa. He stopped, looked back, scratched his head, and drawled, "Boy, I'm sure glad I didn't do that in the house!"

Goldfield

GOLDFIELD, FORTY MILES north of Gold Point, was a wild place in the early 1900s. The town held thirty thousand people, had five newspapers, three railroads, a hundred whorehouses, and saloons twenty-five to the

Although Goldfield, Nevada, is not entirely deserted, a number of very substantial buildings, like this four-story brick and stone hotel, have been long vacant.

block. Gold was pouring from the ground, and high-grading paid better than wages.

High-grading became a way of life, or at least a way to the good life. Miners had special pockets sewn into their coveralls, and wore shoes with hollow heels and soles. Even pick handles were hollowed out and cleverly plugged. Mine owners, figuring half of the best ore was walking out of the mines, insisted on building change houses so that no clothing or tools would leave the premises. The miners' union fought the move, and eventually federal troops were called in to cool things down.

By 1918, the veins were running thin, causing the big operator, Goldfield Consolidated, to close down. The town lost

Santa Fe Club of Goldfield, Nevada, has catered to miners for eighty years. Business was good when miners could trade chunks of "high grade" for drinks.

Charlie Cecchini, the ranking old-timer of Goldfield, and storyteller extraordinary.

half of its population. Tex Rickard closed up his saloon and hung a sign on the door, "God has gone to Rawhide." Then in 1923, a whiskey still blew up and much of the town burned, with the help of a fifty-mile-per-hour wind.

Charlie Cecchini was the ranking old-timer in Goldfield. He had lived there for sixty-one years when we visited a few years ago. He is a delightful old fellow, and a great story-teller. Give him a chance to light his pipe, and he'll crinkle his eyes, take a breath, and tell it straight out.

The fire in 1923 burned him out, and he had to buy an-other house. Things were cheap, since most of the population had moved out, so Charlie got his new house for twenty dol-lars down and twenty dollars a month until the entire pur-chase price of eighty dollars was paid off. He was earning six dollars a day mining for the Spearhead Mine. Later he worked for other mines, was constable, and for a while worked as a railroad engineer. It was during that time that a fellow engineer drove his train through a house.

This story called for a new fill of tobacco and three kitchen matches to get it fired properly. Talking through clenched teeth, and with an old country accent, Charlie began his story.

"I was the engineer of a long train about a hundred miles outa here, near the town of Mina. Had about 150 cars on a sidetrack. Goldfield said they would send help, another engine, and two guys to help me out. They came puffing in at 3:30 A.M. with two-by-fours hanging all over the engine, and parts of a porch stuck on the headlight. It seems the two guys fell asleep on the way and didn't wake up 'til they ran through the house. The house had been moved to a spot by the tracks, ready to be loaded and relocated. Seems the wind blew the house onto the tracks, just in time for the engine to smack it dead center."

Charlie struck another match and continued. "The engineer lost his leg when lumber flew through the cab. And lost his job when the boss caught up with him."

Charlie Cecchini must be pushing eighty by now. I hope he is still puffing away and telling those grand stories through clenched teeth.

Ione, Berlin and Grantsville

SOMEWHERE NORTH OF TONOPAH and east of
the highway, an old road winds its way to three little
ghost towns, Ione, Berlin, and Grantsville. Ione had an old
log building with a fine sod roof that sprouted a tall crop of
shady greenery. Just south, the remains of the old Berlin
Mill were now surrounded by the grounds of Ichthyosaur
State Park.

Grantsville, the only town of the three that captured my
attention, was obviously named after General Ulysses S.
Grant. It was located at the head of Grantsville Canyon,

Mill ruins on the left, mess hall and kitchen on the right, with old brick schoolhouse
at mid-distance, make up the remains of Grantsville, Nevada.

with Grantsville Ridge on one side and Sherman Hill on the other. The town's sympathies were blatant, and few rebel sympathizers ever admitted their preference.

An old mill, a blown safe, a brick school, and a number of shacks sat on the west side of town. A sod-roofed rock house and one-half of an adobe outhouse made up the remainder of what was once the largest town in the area.

The rock residence had stood for more than a hundred years, owing to its stout construction. The roof ridge was a

Stout adobe outhouse manages an upright stance in spite of losing two walls. Note tall vent for odor-free operation.

twelve-by-twelve timber, as was the rather unnecessary center pole. The little adobe outhouse was of equal strength, as evidenced by the fact that it still stood firm despite the loss by vandalism of two of its walls. The roof was intact, extending outward in cantilever fashion, and extending three feet above the roof, the cesspool ventilator still delivered untoward odors to the passing breeze.

Humbolt

GHOST TOWNS are great fun to visit. On those occasions when an old-timer still sits in residence, it can be fascinating. When two bachelor brothers hold down the remains, it can be hilarious

Such was the case several hundred miles northeast of Reno, near the Rye Patch Reservoir, where Bill and Tom James guard the history of Humbolt town and Humbolt House. They were seventy and seventy-four years old when I visited them a few years ago, but spry as fifty, and as full of the devil as a pair of teenagers.

When I first asked their names, they answered in turn, "I'm W. T. — Bill James," and "I'm T. H. — Tom James." Their formality belied their sincere hospitality. They loved history, enjoyed recounting stories, and had pat answers for the most obvious questions.

"We are no relation to the James boys — Jesse and the gang, but our grandfather once provided a hideout for Jesse."

As to the old town of Humbolt, they had no firsthand information, but they'd talked to Charlie Owens, the first resident of Humbolt, and could tell me what Charlie had said. Bill led off.

"Old Charlie was eighty in 1920. He always called the town a highly tooted place. They mined silver there — began in 1860, when Charlie was sixteen, then got to be a real town in '68." Tom listened carefully, and lent support with a nod of the head.

"There was more than a hundred buildings up there —

W. T. (Bill) James, and T. H. (Tom) James, guardians of Humbolt, Nevada, history.

long one's still there — the old Wells Fargo Bank — but Charlie says fifteen of 'em was whorehouses. Said there was three saloons."

I asked if there were any churches or schools. Tom shook his head as Bill continued. "Charlie never mentioned any. 'Course he was pretty old."

Bill paused, thinking, then cracked a broad grin and told about the famous gunfight the way old Charlie had told it to him.

"Three guys in the saloon was arguing, and they got kinda mad about it. They all had cap and ball Colts in their belts, and pretty soon their hands were edgin' toward the handles. Everyone but the three angry guys hit the deck or

Somewhere among these ruins of Humbolt was the saloon where a shootout left no survivors.

ran outside." Bill's eyes started sparkling as he recalled the good part of the story.

"Charlie says one man went right over the top of him, goddam sunabitch, he wasn't just a runnin', he was flyin'!"

Now Bill's voice has gone up a notch, and Tom is leaning forward as if he had never heard the story before.

"Blam, Blam, Blam — and then it went awful quiet! The room was full of smoke from the black powder, but when it cleared, here come more bystanders, crawlin out, and inside, all three of those guys was dead!"

The James boys keep a neat house and yard, although the yard is full of remnants of their considerable past. An old grease rack was built to service their 1915 Ford truck that

The open door of this Humbolt outhouse invites; the sign denies. Use this facility with mixed feelings.

they bought in 1938 for five bucks. When it broke down, they tore out the engine and powered the sawmill that stands off to the side. They owned a number of Model T's, apparently storing the old ones as they bought new ones. Recently, they sold the old wrecks off. "Got five hundred dollars for the last one," says Bill.

An old wooden propeller, bolted to one of the outbuildings, raised my curiosity. Bill was pleased I had noticed it.

"From a De Haviland mail plane. Used to come over here before we built the place — started in 1919, always flew two-wingers. Wouldn't trust those single-wingers." Tom silently agreed, then pointed north as Bill continued.

"Used to be a schoolhouse up north aways. Mail pilots flyin' those De Havilands would come down and fly low right over the school. Kids would all flood out and wave. The pilot always waved back."

He paused and looked over at the propeller. "One of the pilots was killed in a crash, and another pilot — I guess it was his friend, flew over to drop a wreath, and he crashed too!"

A few years after my visit with the James boys, I flew my newly completed red and white biplane down the right side of the railroad track on my way to the Reno National Air Races. I roared over the James boys' place, then circled about and waved from the open cockpit. Down below, two figures stepped out of the house and waved back.

Part IX – California

Johnsville (Jamison)

IF A TWO-STORY OUTHOUSE existed in California, it would probably be high up at the head waters of some gold-bearing creek. I traveled up the Trinity, down the Trinity, up the Klamath, the Salmon, and numerous small streams — wherever a road granted access. There were countless small towns with neither spectacular outhouses nor memorable stories. I'm not even sure I could find the towns again. Places like Calahan and Cecilville fade into obscurity, but Johnsville was memorable.

Once called Jamison, the town of Johnsville, now protected by the boundaries of Plumas Eureka State Park, lies ninety miles as the crow flies north, and a bit east of Sacramento. From 1850 to 1890, Johnsville was a noted gold mining town, but as the ore pinched out, recreational skiing took its place. In fact, skiing, called snowshoeing at the time, became popular in 1869, causing most historians to consider the slopes along Jamison Creek to be the birthplace of recreational skiing in America.

Placer gold was found in the creek in 1850, but soon after, prospectors found the hard rock mother lodes on the slopes above. During the next twenty years, numerous mining operations were developed, capitalized, sold, and resold. None seem to have been operated efficiently. In 1872, English interests bought up most of the mines and created an orderly, money-making operation. The superintendent of operations was named William Johns, so the new town, built to replace Jamison Town, was called Johnsville.

At the peak of operations, the largest mill ran sixty

Mohawk Mill lies to the east of Johnsville, California. Sixty stamps of 600 pounds lifted eight inches and dropped in turn, crushing 150 tons of ore per day.

stamps, processing 150 tons of ore per day, from which one thousand dollars in bullion was claimed every twenty-four hours.

Also, three "chile" or "chili" wheels ground lesser amounts of ore. Each wheel was a pair of nine-foot-diameter, two-foot-thick granite rollers that wheeled about like two unicyclists' arms locked, peddling in opposite directions.

Snow fell seven months of the year, and to deliver ore, snow sheds were constructed over ore car tracks, or tramways were built to connect mine and mill. Perhaps it was the presence of the tramways that brought about the popularity of snowshoeing. Miners could sling their twelve-foot "shoes" over their shoulders and hitch a ride up the hill on one of the three tramways, then ski down and do it again. Two of the tramways were more than fifteen hundred feet long.

Recreational enthusiasts once claimed fights were the most popular endeavor, followed by women, then fights over women, jumping, foot races, and snowshoeing. But after the trams were built, the preference was reversed.

In 1869, flyers advertised: "Four Days of Snowshoe Races, and a Grand Ball on St. Patrick's Night."

That was only the beginning. In 1871, a reporter described the races, as later published in the Plumas County Historical Society's, "Plumas Memories."

> ... The event was a snow-shoe race of three miles, for a purse of two hundred dollars, the contestants being four of our cit-

Hotel and firehouse in the town of Johnsville. Town was named after William Johns, superintendent of combined mining operations.

izens, viz: Mr. Chris Kennan, "a wearing of the green," Mr.
Frank Surratt, with scarlet colors, against Mr. Louis Christopher, with crimson, and Mr. Chas. Hanson, in blue, the citizens making a purse in addition, of fifty dollars, to be given to
the second man in. . . .

. . . At the signal all started in fine style, Kennan and Surratt
gaining rapidly for about a thousand yards, when Surratt, in
passing a tree, broke a shoe and came down, Kennan running
upon him and also coming down, with a shoe broken. Hanson
added his body to the pyramid, but was soon on his shoes
again, while Christopher steered clear, and for a moment had
the race all to himself; but Hanson soon came up to him upon
a steep pitch, and the two came between the poles, Christopher in ten and a half minutes, and Hanson fifteen seconds
later, winning both purses.

Experts, who were upon the ground, say that with shoes and
snow both in excellent order, the distance could be made in
seven minutes. The snow, yesterday, was too wet for fast time.

Kennan and Surratt, Although defeated, are not dismayed,
and challenged any parties living in the Jamison Mining District to a race over the same course for any sum, from $250 to
$500 a side. . . .

In 1872, the race course was shortened to 1676 feet, no
doubt matching the length of one tramway.

. . . McDonald led off, gaining forty feet on his competitor, but
in crossing the flat Hanson came up finely, and at forty feet
from the outcome one of his shoes passed between those of
McDonald, and of course it was all up with Hanson. Here
Hanson made a pass with his pole at the shoes of his opponent,
but punched the rider in the head instead, and Mc, in return,
threw his pole at Hanson who raised up on his shoes to grasp
Mc by the shoulder, losing his balance and going between the
poles somewhat like a catharine-wheel in a Fourth of July celebration, Mc winning the purse. Time, 25 seconds. . . .

. . . Then came Kennan and John Penman. The start was a
good one, but on the turn of the long pitch, Penman inadver-
tently permitted the point of his pole to touch, which caused it

to fly from his grasp, hitting him a hard blow on the back of his head, with force enough to send the pole flying twenty feet into the air. This staggered him for an instant and caused him to run wide, and lose about forty feet, but recovering his position he came in splendidly, only four feet behind his opponent. Time, 24 seconds. . . .

In the small museum near the old Mohawk Mill, one can see some of the ten-foot and twelve-foot skis used by the old-time snowshoers, and read about the deeds of the most famous skier of the time, Snow Shoe Tompson. For five years, Snow Shoe skied the mail from Placerville to Genoa and back, taking

From *Helldorados, Ghosts and Camps of the Old Southwest*

The longest single-span wooden covered bridge in the United States, and probably the world. Structure was recently declared a California Historical Landmark.

fifteen days for each round trip, a feat that would be hard to duplicate today.

Downhill and southwest of Johnsville, in much gentler clime, one of the early settler's most spectacular creations still spans the Yuba River after more than one hundred years of continuous use. It is said to be the world's longest wooden covered bridge, with a free span of 230 feet. I had driven its length some years earlier, and being in the vicinity, I wished to drive within its shadowed timbers once more in celebration of man's engineering skills.

But alas, a new concrete bridge, shortly upstream, had replaced the old structure, and the covered bridge was closed to traffic.

Reinforcements and supporting pillars had been added, some of which seemed poorly designed, and almost guaranteed to wipe out the bridge should high water cause debris to gather.

Camptonville

DURING MY WANDERINGS in the California outback, I stumbled upon a combination of enterprises quite new and unexpected. It was a small country store with a cafe in the back that served as a bar in the evenings.

I had breakfast in Bill "Bull" Meek's place in Camptonville, and it was an order of magnitude beyond. Beyond what? Well, beyond strangeness is the best way to put it — and I guess you would have to understand the Clampers to really know the meaning of strange. Bill Meek was a Head Humbug of the E. Clampus Vitus organization, and his outlook on life could be seen in his unique store.

The front of the large two-story building was mostly grocery store. A cubicle on the left enclosed the Justice Court, and was occupied by Meek's grandson, Acton Cleveland. In the back, a heavy-duty bar stretched across the width of the building. To the side were three refrigerators filled with beer, and in the corner leaned a baseball bat and an axe handle.

It was 9:00 A.M. and the man cooking my breakfast alternated between sucking on a cigar and sipping a beer. Somewhere a juke box was running on low. Two unshaven characters entered on a zigzag course, bumped into me and apologized. The cook eyed them carefully, then checked the corner to see that the weapons were handy. The two sat down, arguing heavily. The cook reached under the cash register, grabbed a billy club and slammed it on the counter, eyed the two men and asked, "Would you gentlemen care to order?"

Camptonville was originally a gold mining town, cater-

J. R. Meek's combination grocery, cafe, bar and justice court served the public for
seventy-five years in Camptonville, California.

ing to the needs of the placermen, and later the hydrau-
lickers. Town was moved twice to permit sluicing the land
for gold. At its peak, there were more than fifteen hundred
people, and thirty stores, hotels and saloons, stretched out on
both sides of a mile-long plank road. Later, when the gold
was gone, the town dwindled, but survived on the logging
industry.

The old country store had been burned to the ground and
rebuilt twice, the last time with concrete blocks. Even that
building burned down recently, and its customers were taken
over by the bar across the street.

Much of the town's history is tied in with the strange

Small version of the Pelton wheel displayed on monument in Camptonville. Monument was erected by the hell-raising E. Clampus Vitus Brotherhood.

group mentioned earlier — the E. Clampus Vitus, which in Latin means something like 'from darkness to light.'

The Clampers, as described by one of their own members, were a bunch of horseplaying, jackass-braying men dedicated to the burlesque of all secret societies, and to the preservation of the belly laugh and heavy drinking. It was charitable on occasion, always claiming to help widows and orphans, mostly the former. They believed in exercising reverence for womanhood, even while in pursuit.

Meetings were held anywhere, preferably in bars, but if outside, the meeting place was called the Hall of Comparative Oration. They proved that men will be boys!

The society began in West Virginia as a hoax and a joke, and traveled to the West, gathering mystique on the way. Joe Zumwalt carried the idea to California, and the garb he habitually wore became the uniform of future Clampers. Joe wore long red-flannel underwear, no shirt, a rope belt, dungarees, old boots, and a plug hat. Heading parades as the Grand Humbug, he also carried a ten-foot staff with a phallic symbol on top.

Parades were frequent — sometimes nightly — or whenever a few new conscripts could be conned into joining. The fee varied from nothing to "half of what you have." Initiates were blindfolded, stripped to their long underwear, smeared with cream or butter, or whatever could be found, then paraded down the street. Once accepted, they had the honor of buying drinks for older members for the balance of the evening, and sometimes part of the next day.

The Clampers have carried out some worthwhile projects, such as designating the long covered bridge on the Yuba as a National Historic Civil Engineering landmark. They also placed a plaque honoring Lester Allen Pelton, inventor of the Pelton wheel. The wheel enabled water to be used efficiently to power such things as stamp mills.

Tiny jail seldom saw service. Hasp apparently used a nut and bolt locking system.

Part X – Oregon

Cornucopia

FORTY MILES EAST of Baker, Oregon, at the little town of Halfway, a road exits to the left and soon becomes a climbing winding gravel road reaching into the Wallowa Mountains, ending at the old mining town of Cornucopia. It was a good prospect for a tall outhouse, owing to its altitude, but a search of the town revealed no such structure. I would have crossed it off my list as a failure had I not been taken with the beautiful architecture and excellent workmanship evident in the construction of some of the buildings. Two old homes were particularly beautiful, with vaulted roof lines, fancy windows, arched balconies, and nicely angled staircases. Even some of the old tumbled and torn wrecks seemed to take on a noble character as they leaned into the elements and fought the good fight against the inevitable tug of gravity.

Many of the buildings were built during the first boom in 1884, when the population peaked at about one thousand. All had high-peaked roofs to shed the heavy snowfall that often exceeded twenty-four feet. Roads became snowpacked to a depth of eight feet, and stage coaches ran on sled runners instead of wheels. It was a cold place in the winter, and cold all year round in some of the mines.

The names of some of the claims indicate the nature of the weather and the climate down the shafts and tunnels. "Alaska," "Van Winkle," "Arctic," and "Bruin," were a few.

Extensive remains of one of these mines can be found at the edge of town. Most of the buildings are intact, including a structure at the mine entrance. On the tracks exiting the mine are a dozen side-tipping ore cars, a personnel car, and an old rusty engine. Considerable water flows from the mine opening and becomes a good-sized creek that flows through town. Stepping into the mouth of the tunnel, one is met by a blast of cold air.

A short distance from the tunnel, a large two-story building served as a bunkhouse for unmarried miners. It had six rooms upstairs and four down; the central recreation room

Miner's classy little house in Cornucopia, Oregon, now an even classier vacation home, sported a diamond window and outside stairway to upper floor.

Mine structures adjacent to the Coulter Tunnel, where ice-cold air and ice-cold water pour forth.

had a large stove in the middle, the building's only source of heat.

A small building next door holds an old wagon bed equipped with ten-foot runners, making this a sled shed. Next door is the old mine office, plastered with maps and complete with receipts from 1940, obviously the date of the last mining effort.

One of the rooms in the mine office had a door somewhat shorter than normal. This opened to a throne room complete with elevated floor and john. It was Sir John Harrington that gave the "john" its name, just as Sir Thomas Crapper provided us the "crapper" — two inventors seldom given credit for their widely used creations.

Homestead

DROPPING DOWN OUT of the mountains, I took a left at Halfway and headed for the Snake River and the town of Homestead. My topographic maps and outdated maps of mining districts had revealed dozens of likely towns. Any town that looked like a going concern on an old map, and is barely indicated, or better yet, missing entirely on new maps, was the sort of place I wanted to have a look at.

Most such towns had kept up with the times, destroying old buildings and replacing them with new structures which, of course, were built with no thought of outhouses or the preservation of history.

Homestead was an exception. Located on the confluence of Pine Creek and the Snake River, at the lower end of Oxbow Lake, this mining remnant had two old but well kept homes, and dozens of old weathered buildings — just the type of installation that I enjoyed. Nosing about the buildings, I could deduce their past roles, perhaps gain an idea of what brought them into existence, and what caused their demise.

One old building looked like a school, and indeed still had slates on the walls. Checking the copyright date on some old books indicated the school probably closed in the forties. On a shelf in the coal house behind the school, I found a 1931 reader. I stood there, with two cameras slung about my neck, scanning the old book, when the elderly caretaker confronted me.

The caretaker wasn't sure what he should do with me.

Large schoolhouse in Homestead, Oregon, evidences the great number of families who once lived in the now deserted company town.

He looked me over, eyed the cameras, and told me not to take anything. I agreed, and we went our separate ways.

An old road led up the hill a short distance to a deserted mine and mill. Bits of blue rock were scattered throughout the waste dump, indicating copper was mined at one time. The place was littered with old machinery and belts. At the mine opening, a number of ore cars sat on a short stretch of rails, resting on rotted ties. An old ledger showed the name "Iron Dyke Mine," and listed the assay on one shipment. The ore was heavy in copper and contained a small amount of gold.

I returned to the largest building in what must have been a company town. It was over one hundred feet long, perhaps half as wide, and had a broad covered porch running its full length. Peeking through the windows, I could see dining halls, pastime rooms, and a large kitchen. Reaching the end of the large building, I was surprised to find it was joined to another building of similar size and construction.

Somewhere nearby I could hear voices — loud voices, raised to overcome impaired hearing.

"Well, if you caught him in the school, why didn't you throw him out?"

"Well, I ragged him a while, then told him not to steal anything."

Obviously the two gentlemen were hired as caretakers, and probably lived in the two well kept homes along the row. It wouldn't do to leave them in doubt.

I found them just around the corner, and turning up my volume, I let them know that I was about to leave the place.

Dining halls, pastime rooms, and probably bunkhouses for single miners of the Homestead Mine Company.

They relaxed, their problem solved, even seemed friendly. Indeed, they supplied answers to all my questions.

The place once held one hundred families, and enough single miners to fill both dormitories. The original claim was made in 1890, but the mining hit its peak between 1915 and 1918, then again from 1925 to 1927, but most of the mines closed in 1942. That's when the school locked its doors.

More than 150 men worked in the Iron Dyke Mine alone, and some mining was carried out there until 1952. The company provided its workers with two stores and a choice of several saloons!

The entire operation was presently owned by the Butler Ore Company, the employer of the two caretakers.

I offered them a cup of coffee out of my thermos, or a beer from the icebox, but was politely refused. Obviously that would be exceeding the bounds of proper behavior for caretakers charged with protecting the grounds from the likes of me.

Part XI – Idaho

Wallace and Murray

F OR THE PAST few months, wherever I traveled, someone always suggested I visit Silver City, Idaho. A few folk had suggested the area north of Kellogg and Wallace, Idaho. Again, planning to save the best for last, I headed north into the panhandle of Idaho to have a look at the area near Wallace.

After a while, driving becomes rote and a person's mind tends to wander. I recalled the various reactions that followed my many inquiries concerning two-story outhouses. Most people were dumbfounded, tending to sputter out some sort of stalling answer, waiting for a punch line or an explanation. In Montana and Wyoming there was occasional understanding, and often there were apologies that the structures had all disappeared. In Texas they said, "What?" But in Crested Butte, Colorado, when asked about two-story outhouses, they assumed that you needed to use it! I wondered what the reaction would be in Idaho.

Wallace, located at the east end of "Silver Valley," is a town of about two thousand people, and likes to be known as "The Home of the Silver Dollar." It's the headquarters for a number of mining and smelting companies, and has the gray sooty look of a town long in the mining and smelting business.

The museum in Wallace had a number of excellent ore samples, old photographs, and booklets telling of the long-lasting union wars that racked the community.

From Wallace, a number of roads radiated outward like the spines of a spider's web, reaching upward along various

Looking upstream along Canyon Creek (see text for hints of a more descriptive name) in the town of Burke, Idaho. Peaked roof is schoolhouse.

creeks and gulches. I drove up Nine Mile Road to Delta, then cut over the hill east to the marvelous old town of Murray. The town was full of history and old buildings, but there were few people and no tall outhouses. Everyone said, "Go to Burke."

I returned to Wallace and took the Canyon Creek Road, passing through a nearly continuous series of mines, smelters, and small settlements. Gem blended with Black Bear, which gave way to Mace, and became Burke. Along the way I drove a road that also made up the bed of two railroads, the Northern Pacific and the Oregon Washington lines. Beneath the concrete surface ran the waters of Canyon Creek.

I would soon learn that Canyon Creek was not the proper name for the creek in this locality, but Ripley's claim that this was the only place in the world where the railroad, the creek and the road occupied the same space, was thoroughly evident. In fact, I would find another category that could be added to Ripley's claim.

Burke

I T WAS LATE AFTERNOON, and the only establishment open in the little town of Burke was a bar crowded between the road, railroad, creek, and the rising ground behind. I entered, and soon became educated to the local ways and local terminology.

After ordering a sandwich at the bar, I spread out an old 1901 topographic mining map of the area. Old maps tend to attract a certain type of onlooker — those interested in history, and willing to share their interest. This time it was the barmaid. She left the bar and took up a position where she could read the map over my shoulder.

I took the cue and asked her if there were any two-story outhouses in the vicinity.

"You bet," was the reply. "At least there was one behind the Sweets Hotel up S*** Creek aways."

I pointed out the creek on the map. "Says here the stream is called 'Canyon Creek.'" Her reaction was unexpected.

"Hey, Joe — Come here — look at this map. They got the name of S*** Creek wrong. You ever hear it called Canyon Creek?"

Joe answered from across the room. "Hell, no. It's always been S*** Creek — long as I can remember, anyhow."

That particular four-letter word had never been in my mixed company repertoire, and I was slightly embarrassed to hear it shouted about. I expected every head in the place to swivel in my direction in mild disapproval. But not a head turned. I was the one that was out of step, and badly outnumbered. So be it.

The George Gulch outhouse-bridge combination of Burke, Idaho. It may be the only such structure in existence.

Indeed, the creek was an open sewer. Outhouses emptied into the creek from both sides for a mile upstream. There were overhangers, trestle jobs, creek straddlers, and on a small tributary called "George Gulch" (I wasn't about to ask

Typical creek-drop attached outhouse common to most homes along the waterway. The residents' regularity was public knowledge, of course.

Rear view of bridge-outhouse implies a community use by residents of several homes.

the local name), there was a bridge–outhouse combination. I had thought I knew it all when it came to unusual outhouses, but the bridge combo was new and fascinating.

The bridge was wood, a single span of about twenty feet, wide enough for one car and two outhouses, that joined in the center to become one long structure accessed by two doors. The road crossing the bridge led to two unpainted homes, and the outhouses were no doubt a part of the property. I photographed the structure from all angles, noting that the

The bridge portion of the combo is wide enough and stout enough to handle cars and light trucks.

This creek drop, self-flushing outhouse required a small diversion dam to course water under the drop zone.

sun was at the wrong angle. I would have to return for the morning light.

There was a nice place to pull off and camp a few miles up the main creek, just above the intake for the town's water supply. A sign nearby prohibited construction of any buildings (meaning outhouses in particular) upstream from that point.

I dug out my maps and pamphlets pertinent to the area and spent the evening learning about the one-hundred-year mining effort in Silver Valley.

The 1901 map showed a number of mines that are not indicated on later maps. Obviously those mines were short-lived. The 1939 and 1957 maps indicated that Dorn split off from Black Bear, then both faded into their neighbors, and that Frisco was born near Gem. The Oregon Washington line changed to the Union Pacific, and the town of Burke grew another half mile up of what all three maps referred to as Canyon Creek.

The "Sneaky Pete" model is guaranteed to provide the ultimate in privacy. Just where the back door once led is a mystery.

Above Burke were the Tiger–Poorman Mine, the Hercules, Tamarack, Custer, and Neversweat Mines.

Gold had been found in the area about 1860, but large-scale mining did not occur until the 1880s. In 1892, the fights between mine owners and organized miners began. The first battle resulted in sixteen wounded and five dead before the army was called in. But the miners' union had a foothold.

Dissatisfaction with working conditions continued for several years, and another war broke out in 1899. Over one hundred miners commandeered a train, loaded it with dynamite, and forced the engineer to drive it west to Kellogg. They parked the train under the Bunker Hill Mill and set it off! Two men were killed by gunfire, and the army returned to restore order. More than twelve hundred miners were arrested.

Slowly the gold gave out, and zinc, silver, and lead became the production metals. Lead refining in the valley spread its own slow insidious cancer. The accidental target was the health of the populace, primarily the children.

Lead poisoning had been discounted for years until it was found that the children in the schools had a high lead content in their blood. This caused damage to the nervous system, and a general reduction in learning ability.

The next morning I headed down the valley, cameras loaded and ready. Most of the homes along the creek had extensions that hung over the creek, or outbuildings that straddled the creek.

Later, I learned that a whorehouse once stood on the creek bank, and a level catwalk extended to an outhouse that stood over the creek on twenty-foot stilts. It was an older gentleman from Northport who told me about it.

"Used to go to work in the morning shift, 'bout four in the morning — still kinda dark. That's when the gals were finished workin' and doin' their chores out back. We used to applaud each one when they walked the catwalk back of the cathouse. Sometimes they'd take a bow. We applauded everything, including the sound effects."

He looked at me carefully, and watched me take notes.

"Tell ya who ya ought to talk to about them gals." He paused. "No — No — I won't give the old S.O.B. the satisfaction."

The light was right, and I returned to the bridge-outhouse for more photographs. The resident of one of the homes watched me from his window. He saw me snap photos, then write in my notebook. Soon he came to the conclusion that I was a government man gathering evidence, probably a member of the hated Environmental Protection Agency.

He rushed out of the door, ran to the bridge and hollered, "We don't use it anymore. Ya hear? We ain't used it for mor'n a year!"

Silver City

DRIVING SOUTH, headed for Silver City, I passed through a number of towns that looked great on the old maps, but none of them suited my purpose. Near Idaho City, I detoured to the remains of the Golden Age Camp to see whether the little outhouse with the big sign over the door still survived. It did — the sign read, "MAIN EN-TRANCE."

Silver City is most easily reached via Jordan Valley, Oregon. A more challenging entrance is by way of the twen-ty-two-mile lumpy gravel road from State Highway 45, south of Boise. Either way, the town is well worth visiting; more than seventy buildings are still intact.

Overview of Silver City, Idaho, looking north. The Idaho Hotel is at center left, butcher shop, Leonard's Store and Barber Shop line up on the near right.

From *Ghost Towns of the Northwest*

And where is the exit?

The old War Eagle Hotel had a very tall two-story outhouse, but hotel and house burned down some years ago. However, a large number of tall specimens are still in action.

The Masonic hall, once a wood milling shop, built astraddle Jordan Creek, has two outhouses attached to the flank so as to drop deposits directly into the creek. A city ordinance later prohibited its use except during flood stage, at which time it was recommended that all trash be thrown in the creek, and the deposits in all earth closets be shoveled out and disposed of the same way. Sort of a huge annual flushing!

In 1866, the big town in the area was Ruby City, with a population of almost a thousand people. The first winter, snow drifted so badly that some folk moved a mile south, upstream, to a more sheltered spot. Within two years, everyone had skidded their homes and stores, with the aid of sled runners and oxen, to the new site, and Silver City was born.

The Tidal Wave was published as the town's first paper. Later it became the *Owyhee Avalanche,* a daily paper. At its peak, with somewhere between twelve hundred and five thousand population, the town had six stores, two hotels, a brewery,

Baling wire holds the splayed bottom of this tall outhouse together.

and nine saloons, six of which were known to be Hurdy Gurdys. The Hurdy Gurdy joints stood in a row and became known as "Virgin's Alley."

About this time, two prospectors filed a claim on a prospect

Walkway to outhouse may have been wider at one time. Now it gives a one-door option only.

This walk-through style tall house is behind the tin shop and newspaper office. Proximity to the creek, which runs under the Masonic hall just behind, made the annual spring cleanout a cinch.

later to be called the Poorman Mine. Then another man claimed an outcrop of the same vein about one thousand feet away.
He was challenged by the original claimants, then ousted by a
third group who promptly built a fort at the tunnel entrance.
They called it Fort Baker and held off any claim jumpers.
Later, all the purported owners sold out, and the new owners
promptly took out $2 million worth of gold and silver.

Masonic hall of Silver City, Idaho, straddles Jordan Creek. Note the attached outhouses
that drop into the creek.

Idaho Hotel is still "in business," catering to tourists, offering guided tours and refreshments.

The Oro Fino Mine was so rich that the ore could be crushed by sledge and panned by hand. Its ore ran more than $6 thousand of silver per ton of ore.

Most of the ore was very rich and easily processed. Four stamp mills in town had only a total of fifty stamps, yet nearly $40 million in valuable metals was taken from the area, making the Silver City Lode second only to the Comstock in Nevada.

Mining slacked off in the '80s, then surged again in 1930. Silver City lost its place as county seat in 1934, and by 1944 only one man, Willie Hawes, was left in town. Willie, who died in 1968 at age ninety-one, was responsible for the town's preservation during the twenty-some years that Silver City had become a ghost.

Silver City's history was marked by several large-scale shoot-outs. When a dispute over claim boundaries could not be resolved, each side hired gunslicks. The Golden Chariot Mine crew attacked the Ida Elmore group, and fought a gun battle for three days. Many were wounded, but only two were killed — one from each side — before the cavalry arrived to break it up. The fight was revived in town, and two more were killed.

The gun fight occurred near the Idaho Hotel, which stands today very much as it did in the 1860s. Three stories tall, and

Fanciest residence in Silver City was the Stoddard house. Stoddard was a mine investor, sawmill owner, and rancher.

Well kept and still used, this outhouse has been patched and repatched with whatever material was at hand.

full of small rooms crowded with furniture, it is the prize tourist spot in town. Where rooms once were two dollars a night, and fire in the room was extra, you can now take a guided tour of the hotel for a similar fee. Ed Jagels, of Murphy, Idaho, the present owner and proprietor, escorts hundreds of visitors through the labyrinthine hallways of the hotel each season. He's full of stories about the town. One of his favorites deals with the hanging of 1881.

When Henry McDonald was found guilty of murder and sentenced to hang, one of the stores in town prepared for the big event by preparing a "Hangman's Special Lunch." It was raining when they transported McDonald to the scaffold. On the way, a youngster ran, slipping and sliding, past the death wagon.

"Goin' somewhere?" asked McDonald.

There's a message here somewhere.

The youngster shouted there was "going to be a hanging."

"No hurry, son — won't be much doin' till I get there," replied McDonald.

Father Nattini and the sheriff soon led Henry McDonald up the steps to the platform and centered him over the trapdoor. The death warrant was read to the victim, his hands were tied, and his head covered with a hood.

At 1:54 P.M. the trap was sprung, and three hundred witnesses left en masse for the saloons.

Part XII – Wyoming

Teapot Dome

WHEN THE PRICE of gasoline rose above a buck a gallon, I cut my travels short until the billfold shock slowly wore off. As a result, I learned a great deal more about Wyoming.

History is close to the surface in my home state. It was here that Jim Bridger hunted, guided, told his lies, and built his fort. Here the Union Pacific cut its ties and forged a path from East to West, in turn receiving title to twenty sections of land for every mile of track laid. And just twenty miles north of my home, the Teapot Dome scandal took place.

When I first visited the Naval Reserve No. 3, called Teapot Dome, I had no idea that a town named Teapot ever existed, but the remains were there — a few old buildings, the remnants of streets, and a grand old water tank. Although chipped by windblown gravel and badly rusted, the words, "Teapot, Wyoming," and "Water Supply" are still quite legible. Just why a water tank would be painted so grandly became clear when I learned the history of the town and the scandal. It would appear that a scam and a scandal were under way at the same time.

Way back in 1873, a Wyoming historian named Hunton, made the journey north from Fort Caspar to investigate rumors of "oily dirt." An Indian guided him and helped him scrape some heavy oil into a container. They had collected almost a quart of "grease" when hostile Indians chased them off.

Many years later, the underground, dome-shaped oil trap was tapped, and in 1920 the dome was declared a naval

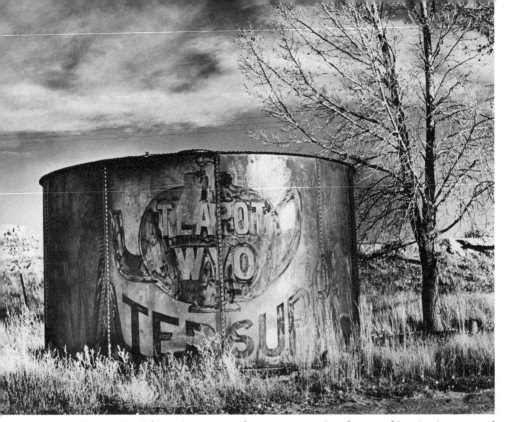

Fancy paint job on the water tank was meant to lure buyers of lots in the proposed town of Teapot, Wyoming.

oil reserve. About this time, President Harding appointed Albert Bacon Fall, formerly a senator from New Mexico, as secretary of interior. In 1922, Secretary Fall contacted Harry Sinclair, president of Mammoth Oil Company, and after receiving $198 thousand in bribes, secretly leased the Teapot Dome to Sinclair. Later, Fall conned Sinclair out of another $64 thousand, then $10 thousand more, and yet another $25 thousand. It bordered on blackmail.

At the same time, the Teapot Development Company erected the water tank, painted it up fancy, and marked off 1,040 town lots. Two hundred seventy-five were sold the first day, and in three months, 903 had been purchased. A store was built, but few lot owners built, preferring to sit on their deeds, hoping that oil rights went with the lots.

When the scandal broke, the town died, if indeed it had

Teapot never amounted to much — a house or two, a number of oil wells, and some basic refining equipment.

ever lived. None of the lot owners profited, but Sinclair and Fall did quite well.

The trial was to take over six years. Several majority stockholders of other oil companies adjourned to France, one

Old wooden oil pumping rig is one of the last in existence. Note the hefty "walking beam" that pivots on the top of the vertical timber.

for twenty-five years, another for the rest of his life. There were two civil suits, two contempt cases, and eight criminal trials. Harry Sinclair was sentenced to three months in jail for refusing to testify and for jury tampering. Former Secretary Fall was convicted of accepting a bribe, and sentenced to one year in jail — not a bad deal, since he had received more than $400 thousand for his complicity.

The Teapot Dome scandal was only a momentary setback for Sinclair and his oil company. Soon, exploration crews found a number of oil fields, and pipelines laced their way across the state connecting wells to refineries.

Along one of those pipelines, in 1923, a pumping station was built to hasten the flow along, and around that station a

Iron slowly replaced the wooden rig parts. Here the wheels are of iron, but have the same design used in older wooden variety.

small town grew. Residents called it Ferris Junction; others called it Ferris Dome, or just plain Ferris. To the Sinclair company it was Station Three, but whatever its name, it was built in the most hostile spot in the state.

Located just south of the Ferris Mountains, and west of the Seminoe Mountains, amid the sand dunes of the high plains desert, the town suffered from low temperatures and high winds, and those damnable sand dunes continually crawled into town, covering fences, crowding houses, and requiring the constant attention of bulldozers.

Pumping station hastened oil from the well to the refinery. Long deserted, this old pump stands in Ferris, Wyoming, a town that was once called Sinclair Station 3.

Photograph was taken from a partially stabilized sand dune that once approached town on a southwest wind. It will move again, and the houses of Ferris, Wyoming, will be buried.

Airborne sand filtered into every nook and cranny, even piling up in attic spaces to such an extent that ceilings collapsed on dining room tables and carpeted living rooms. The Sinclair company spent thousands of dollars vacuuming every attic in town on a rotating basis.

Finally the sand and wind won the battle. In 1949 the town was abandoned. One recluse remained until 1958, and now the buildings are slowly being covered with sand. Some local ranchers are "liberating" the lumber from the buildings before they are buried forever.

The Pedro Mountains

FIFTY MILES NORTH, tucked into the south end of the Pedro Mountains, there is a delightful little pocket of greenery traced through by a small stream of clear cold water. Sagebrush grows twelve feet tall, and cottonwoods soar above.

This was one of the favorite spots of an Indian tribe that lived in the Pedros. They were an isolated tribe and had little contact with other Indians. In the late 1880s, they were crowded out by the white man's incursions, but they left behind a memento that would cause great confusion and speculation.

Two prospectors found a deposit of graphite above the green glade, and claimed it under the name the Ninety-Six Graphite Mine. They dug into the mountain fifty feet or so, then slanted downward, hoping in vain that the vein would richen and thicken. Their efforts failed, and others tried their luck. Traces of gold were found, but nothing of value was uncovered until one blast opened up an old cave that held the mystery left by the Indians.

On a narrow shelf, high on the side of the cave, was found the tiny mummified body of a human being. He was fourteen inches tall, badly wrinkled, and with a head that lopped over as a beret might fall to one side of a man's head. The mummy was put on display, fees charged, and soon became the only profitable item to be "mined" from the Pedros.

Occasionally the mummy was permitted examination by experts, and some not so expert. The results were disappointing to the displayers, and they chose to include in their brochures only those few explanations that made the mummy out to be the remains of a midget Indian. Probably a member of a midget tribe, they claimed. They called it the Little Man, and the Old Ninety-Six Graphite Mine, and every mine within ten miles became the Little Man Mine. Writers perpetuated the mystery, making hay from the story, just as the carnival folk made money displaying the remains for the price of a ticket. The legend grew.

The truth is less exciting. One of the first to examine the mummy was Dr. Whiston, a Casper, Wyoming bone specialist. From X-rays and a general examination, he stated the mummy was the remains of a malformed Indian child, probably the result of inbreeding. The skull was incomplete, allowing the brain to lop over, a rare, but not unknown birth

Headquarters of the Little Man Mine as it became known after the discovery of a mummified Indian baby in a nearby cave.

defect. Such a defect was always fatal soon after birth. Very likely the mother of the malformed infant lovingly placed her child on the high ledge in the cave, then closed the opening with rock. Time and dry air aged the child. The wrinkles and a little imagination created the legend of the Little Man, and an entire race of pygmy Indians.

Independence Rock

AT THE TURN of the century, when Cattle Kate left Rawlins and homesteaded a small spread on the Oregon Trail near Independence Rock, a series of events were set in motion that would rock the state, and ultimately cost her her life and that of her friend, Jim Averill.

Kate had a reputation for trading personal favors, and seemed to have a working agreement with Averill, who ran a store and saloon situated a mile from Kate's, near the Sweet Water River. After an evening of boozing it up at Averill's, a celebrating cowboy would be pointed in the direction of Kate's cabin, where he could find satisfaction for a nominal fee. Lacking funds, it became common for cowpokes to trade a maverick calf for Kate's favors. A calf a piece, as it were. Soon she became known as "Cattle Kate."

Kate's herd grew, and in time the number of cattle exceeded what the nearby ranchers considered a reasonable number of motherless, unbranded critters.

Averill sometimes took calves in trade for merchandise, and added them to Kate's herd. Obviously the cowhands considered calves, which they intentionally left unbranded, a sort of fringe benefit.

When Averill led a movement to prevent ranchers from controlling enormous land areas by what he considered illegal means, the ranchers decided to retaliate. Seven of them stopped by Kate's place, intending to teach her a lesson. A fourteen-year-old lad named Gene Crowder, who had been helping Kate, was taken in tow by the ranchers, for fear he would run for help. They met Jim Averill just leaving his place, and at gunpoint loaded him in the wagon with Kate.

The lad, Gene Crowder, got away in the confusion, and ran to Averill's home, where he enlisted the help of Frank Buchanan. Frank followed the abductors at a distance and later told his story. He claimed they stopped at the river and threatened to drown the two of them. Kate wouldn't buy the brag, and called their bluff. They took their hostages on up the river to the top of a small cliff, where they threw a lariat about Jim's neck, and tied the other end to a tree. They tried to get him to jump off the cliff — "Be game, go ahead and jump." Kate kept dodging the noose they tried to put about her neck, but in the end, she was trussed like Averill.

Buchanan, figuring it was getting serious, sent a shot their way and galloped off for help.

When the posse arrived, both Kate and Jim were dangling at rope's end, hanging off the edge of the cliff. The ranchers were arrested and put under a five thousand dollars bond. At the inquest, Buchanan told the whole story, naming names and offering absolute identification. Several of the ranchers admitted their part in the deed, one claiming they only intended to scare the two "rustlers."

It looked like an open-and-shut case, but strange things began to happen. Gene Crowder, the young lad, died of a disease, and Buchanan failed to show up at the trial. He was last seen riding north in a buggy with a new lawyer. Several witnesses to the ranchers' admissions quietly disappeared.

Judge Corn found that the indictment was "not a true bill," and discharged their bonds!

Nine years later, Buchanan's bones were found north of town, his favorite scarf still tied about the fleshness neck.

Signor, Rongis

ONE OF MY old maps showed a town named Signor, while a later map listed the same town as Rongis. An even later map showed both towns, a few miles apart. All were located on the old Rawlins-to-Lander stage road, just one stop north of the Crooks Gap stage station. It was a puzzle that begged a solution.

The Crooks Gap station, a small building of huge logs, still monitored the occasional traffic on the dusty stage road. Rongis was likewise deserted. An old cabin and a broken-down barn marked the spot. Cattle wandered in and out of both buildings, using doorways as rubbing posts.

Ranchers in the area pointed me toward Harold Rogers, curator of the Lander museum.

According to Harold, a gent by the name of Charlie Fletcher, a traveling gambler, stopped by the small ranch settlement of Signor and got a poker game started. Thirty-six hours later he owned the town and the ranch. He promptly turned the letters about, and renamed his town Rongis. Later, Rongis moved two miles to the west, and the old site reverted to Signor.

A search of old county records turned up another strange name change. When developers bought up the old Ried Road ranch, just south of Lander, Wyoming, they incorporated the ranch as the town of "Timbuctoo," hoping the catchy name would attract attention and enhance sales. It didn't. But I visited the site so that I could claim that I had been to Timbuctoo and back in my search for rare outhouses and wild stories!

Rock cavalry barn of Fort Washakie, now a garage for the state highway department, still harbors a ghost that walks the wood floors in cavalry boots, according to some of the men who work there.

An hours drive northwest of Rongis, just north of Lander, Wyoming, the well kept remains of Fort Washakie can be found. Fort Washakie was built at a time when Indian uprisings were greatly feared, but its stout rock blockhouses were never put to use, except as temporary jails. Today the old cavalry stable is used by the state highway department; several employees stoutly claim it is haunted.

On quiet afternoons, right at quitting time, footsteps can be heard coming down the length of the long building. Dogs perk up their ears and whine as they follow the direction of the footsteps. The footfalls are those of a boot-shod cavalryman, and they turn into a small room now used as an office. There, the rocking chair suddenly begins to rock and creak, and dogs leave the room on bent legs with standing hair.

Obviously the story was true, for there was the dog, right there by the chair. And the chair? A rocking chair, of course!

Jim Bridger

JIM BRIDGER built his fortified store in 1842 at the junction of the emigrant trail and the Black Fork of Green River, in what is now southwestern Wyoming. He traded with trappers, Indians and emigrants with equal favor.

When Mormons settled near Salt Lake and encountered Indian resistance, Bridger was blamed for selling powder to the hostiles. In 1853, 150 Mormons in two parties attacked Bridger's fort, forcing him to vacate. A few years later, Bridger visited with President Buchanan and told him of the problem. Buchanan sent in federal troops to retake the fort. They converted it to a military post, paying Bridger six hundred dollars per year rent. In the meantime, Bridger built a ferry across the North Platte River, next to a Mormon ferry. The Mormon ferry let Mormons across free, but double charged all others. Bridger charged Mormons double and let all others across free. They forced each other out of business.

When the Union Pacific built its tracks past Fort Bridger, a small town sprouted, which continued after the fort was abandoned in 1890. However, the real story is not the fort, but the life of Jim Bridger. He was one of the West's great characters.

Born in 1804, and orphaned at thirteen, he headed West. At eighteen, he joined Ashley's fur trappers and made his first trip into the northern Rockies. When Hugh Glass, one of the trappers, was badly mauled by a grizzly, young Jim Bridger and an older fellow named Fitzgerald were assigned the task of standing by Glass until he died. Indians were in the area, fires were risky, and food was short. Glass weakened, but hung on. When he seemed far past recovery, the two men left him and traveled south to safety.

But Hugh Glass recovered, and crawled and scrambled to Fort Laramie, blood in his eye, looking for those who had deserted him. He threatened Jim with his life, then forgave him since he was young and green.

Jim Bridger topped out at more than six feet, walked remarkably erect for a trapper, and saw things with his pale gray eyes that few others could detect. He was never lost, and had an uncanny feel for the weather.

Jim visited Yellowstone Lake when he was twenty-six and watched as two Indians disappeared forever beneath the crust of a hot pool. Later he told friends of the geysers and hot pools, but few believed him. This set Jim to telling wild stories.

They began to call him "Old Gabe" while he was still young. Everyone listened to his wild stories, and many greenhorns believed them.

He told of petrified birds in petrified trees singing petrified songs, and of a large mountain of pure crystal that you could see through. "Took half a day to walk around it." He claimed that he hauled out a chunk big as his arm and had it tested — "Pure Diamond," he claimed. He even took three shots at an elk in that same area, then walked up to bleed it. Turned out the glass mountain was acting like a telescope — "Thet durn elk was twenty-five miles away."

When he had two arrowheads removed from his back in a one-hour operation, without benefit of anesthesia, the doctor couldn't believe the wounds hadn't gotten infected.

"Meat don't spoil in the mountains," Jim explained.

Bridger spoke English, Spanish, some French, and ten Indian tongues, and he told stories in every language.

Once near Lake DeSmet, a small alkali pond at the time, he pointed out the oil seep above, and the coal outcrop below.

"Jes' open up that thar oil seep and run 'er inter the lake

Little remains of Jim Bridger's original fortified store, but many buildings, like this officers' quarters built when the army took over, can be found reconstructed at the site.

— then touch off thet coal, and bile the hull thing down ter soap."

Captain Palms believed him, and so did a famous historian, who relayed this great idea to his rich friends — even printed the fact later.

Jim always claimed the hills were growing, and delighted in pointing out a large boulder, claiming it was only a pebble when he put it there years ago.

He had a fascination for Shakespeare, always identifying heavily with the characters, but always becoming disillusioned with their foul behavior.

After he saw a Shakespearean play at Fort Laramie, he promptly bought a book of plays at the sutler's, and hired a private to read it to him. He loved it until the private got to the point where the two boy princes had their eyes put out. Jim asked the private, "Did he do that?" When the soldier reread the passage, Jim grabbed the book and threw it in the fire — "That's what I think o' him!"

View of distant elk as seen through "Old Gabe's" Crystal Mountain. The pure diamond had a tendency to magnify the elk's image. After shooting the elk, Bridger walked up to bleed, it. "Thet durn elk was twenty-five miles away!"

He never lost his taste for Shakespeare. Once he stopped a train and traded a span of oxen for a copy of a book on Shakespeare. Later he hired a boy at forty dollars a month to read it to him, until the boy got to the story of Richard III. That cooked it — "I ain't listnen ter any more talk of a man who war mean enough to kill his mother!"

One of Jim's favorites was the story of the "Buffalo Dam." Seems he camped on the Platte, below Cottonwood Springs, when a "herd of buffalo came a streamin' down the hill — we corralled the wagons and put the stock inside, lest they be tromped."

The herd plunged into the river, one on top of another. The droves were enormous, miring down and climbing over until they dammed the river — "and the water rose to where the wagons was — came plumb up to the axles, and it were only a little short of washin' us away and drownin' ever' one."

A few years ago, a coal-fired power plant was built half a hundred miles east of historic Fort Bridger, a place Old Gabe loved for its pristine beauty and its air so clear you could "see for three days."

The power company named it the Jim Bridger plant, and ever since, Old Gabe has been turning unmeasured revolutions per minute in his grave.

In fact, the climate near his burial plot in Kansas City has warmed noticeably since the construction of the power plant, no doubt the result of the friction created by his rapid rotation!

Part XIII – Utah

Promontory

SUMMER WAS APPROACHING and it was time I made plans to follow up the leads and hot tips that had accumulated while I had been rummaging about my home state.

Most of the tips to sites in the continental states had already been followed up on. The inaccuracies of these leads were amazing, and did nothing to instill confidence in the sites yet unvisited.

"Go to Alberta," the tipsters said. "There was a two-story outhouse in Lundbreck — and be sure to visit Nordegg." In British Columbia it was Fort Steele, Wildhorse, and Sandon. Then there were rumors about Flin Flon, Manitoba, and a few towns in Saskatchewan.

I laid out a trip that would include the towns in British Columbia and Alberta. Promontory, Utah, site of the completion of the transcontinental railroad was on the route, and I had long been interested in the site.

President Lincoln and General Granville Dodge met and discussed the feasibility of building a transcontinental railroad in 1863, in the middle of the Civil War. One year later, the Pacific Railroad Act was passed, which authorized payment of ten sections of land and a cash bond for each mile of track to be laid. One year later, Lincoln was dead.

In 1866, construction began with the Central Pacific building east from California, and the Union Pacific laying track west from Omaha. The race was on, with the faster track layer taking the king's share. By 1868 it was clear that the roads would meet somewhere in Utah, but since two-thirds of the per-mile pay was awarded for finished grade, both roads built grades far in advance of their tracks. The government had upped the ante to twenty sections of land per mile of road, and the stakes were high.

By the time the actual tracks approached a meeting point, both railroads had built grades more than 150 miles past the actual meeting point. The grades often ran parallel, although in opposite directions — even crossed several times. Rival grading crews thought nothing of setting off powerful explosive charges without warning, as their competitors labored close by.

After much mediation, grade crews were called in and

Central Pacific and Union Pacific tracks met at Promontory by negotiation, but grades ran past each other without joining for hundreds of miles.

the tracks directed toward a meeting point in Promontory, Utah. The tracks were due to join on May 7, 1869, but the trainload of Union Pacific officers was held up by irate, unpaid workers at Piedmont, Wyoming. The men demanded their back wages. With the engine chained to the rails, the president of the Union Pacific saw the light, and telegraphed east for the funds.

The Central Pacific folk had been celebrating for three days, waiting for the Union Pacific, and were in no mood to agree with the Union Pacific plans on just how the ceremony would be carried out. The crowd grew unruly with the delay, so each side drove its own golden spike and its own silver spike. Each was tapped gently into a pre-drilled, specially polished laurelwood tie. Then the spikes and ties were removed.

A real tie was slipped in place, and the honor of driving the last genuine spike was given to the two presidents of the railroads. Stanford of the Central Pacific missed, so Durant of the Union Pacific took a swing. He also missed. Two old-time spike drivers finished the job.

The story of the joining was better than the visit to the actual site. The engines standing in place are not the original engines, or even the right models. They are rented from Paramount Studios at $100 thousand each. In fact, nothing at the site is original, except one sledge and one shovel, which are on display in the small museum. The government plans to have replica steam engines built, at $350 thousand each, but as far as creating a genuine historical monument at Promontory, the U.S. Government has swung and missed.

Part XIV – Canada

BRITISH COLUMBIA

Riondel

AS I DROVE NORTH through Idaho, headed for British Columbia, I wondered how Canadian historical reclamations would stack up against the meager effort put forth at Promontory.

The road paralleling Kootenay Lake in southeastern British Columbia was smooth and relatively free of traffic. I weighed my chances of finding a two-story (or more) outhouse. Snows were bound to be deep, and much of the province seemed to be twenty or thirty years behind the States regarding indoor plumbing. At my last stop for gas, a small station a few miles into British Columbia, I asked the attendant where I might find the men's room. He said there was no men's room, so I asked where I might find the outhouse. He jerked his head toward the backyard — "Oh, anywhere will be all right."

Riondel, a rather modern mining town, at the dead end of British Columbia's Highway 3A, was a ghost in the making. The town was built around one industry — the Bluebell Lead and Zinc Mine. The town boasted a beautiful golf course, modern school, and a complete business district. But the town was dying. Mining was phasing out, and miners were being transferred or laid off.

In two years it would be a ghost town with a golf course and a swimming pool, unless some entrepreneur could continue it as a summer resort.

I drove about the town, inquired about outhouses, and was directed to try the area west of Kaslo.

A free ferry took me across Kootenay Lake, and I headed up the west shore, passed through Kaslo, and took the "H" road up the hill heading west, going upstream along a small creek.

It was almost dark when the rains came. The creek rose quickly, in places covering the road, so that I had to speculate on its exact location. It was one of those white knuckle situations, and it was a great relief to top out at the old mine site called Retallack.

Retallack, Sandon

THERE WAS A LEVEL gravelly spot just off the road, opposite the old mine building. I backed and filled until my rig was level, then cooked supper and sacked out. Weird noises filtered through the sound of rain on the roof. It was musical at times, and strangely human, like a ghost singing a sad lament. I slept poorly.

In the morning I stepped out of the vehicle, and stared down the deep ten-foot shaft I had unknowingly parked beside.

"Pretty close, huh?" said a voice at my elbow. He was white-bearded and white-haired. Called himself White Water Bert.

"Saw ya come in last night. I was listenin' to the radio — wondered if you was goin' to drive her in that hole."

He was a friendly sort. Told me he lived up there all alone — "like to sing along with the radio," he said. He'd invite me to breakfast, but he'd 'et an hour ago." Said "there weren't no tall outhouses around — try Sandon."

The gravel road south to Sandon rides the east bank of a considerable stream, now high and swift from the night's rain. What's left of Sandon is on the west bank. Only remote viewing was possible.

It was nonetheless impressive. Fronting the buildings was a boardwalk and a "board road," built up of heavy timbers. For some distance, the road and the stream occupied the same spot. I scanned the far side with binoculars, looking for unusual structures, then drove down the hill to New Denver, where White Water Bert had said there was a dandy museum.

White Water Bert lives alone amid the vast remains of deserted mine and mill in Retallack, British Columbia.

The museum was tiny, but held fantastic, and sometimes unbelievable information on Sandon.

The town began when Eli Carpenter and four others, calling themselves the "Noble Five," began mining gold, silver, and a lead ore called galena.

A three-story city hall was built in 1900, and soon the town had twenty-three hotels — quite an unbelievable statistic. There were buildings on both sides of the creek, including a cigar factory! An Opera House! A brewery! The population hit twenty-five hundred at the peak, when the mining and skiing booms coincided. A big ski meet was held in 1925 on a slope claimed to be the second largest ski hill in North America.

Frequent floods on Carpenter Creek wiped out the boardwalks and dock-like streets of Sandon, B.C. Fires took most of the remainder.

A number of fires removed most of the residences, and obviously most of the hotels, real or otherwise. Then the floods of 1957 reduced the town to the remnant visible today. Without doubt, tall outhouses existed here, but had either gone up in smoke or down the river.

Fort Steele

FORT STEELE was only eighty air miles from Sandon, but 250 miles and half a day by road. A quick walk about the reconstructed town revealed some impressive structures, but no tall privies.

Nearly a hundred buildings form a rough rectangle about a grassy court with a bandstand at the center. At one corner there is a gigantic waterwheel that was moved from Perry Creek. At the opposite corner is the reconstruction of the Northwest Mounted Police barracks.

The reconstruction was under way, and I spent a pleas-

Fort Steele's central attraction is the museum built to duplicate the original Wasa Hotel.

ant afternoon watching two artisans tailor logs to a perfect fit.

Joe, the older of the two, wore a hard hat, while Don, much the younger, had long hair held in place by a head-band. Quite an odd couple, but they worked marvelously well together. They used only the tools of the time, like broad- and double-bitted axes, an adz or two, augers, hand-saws, and cant hooks. Each log was trimmed, rolled in place, removed, retrimmed, and the process repeated until the log fell in place with only tiny gaps between. These were caulked later, as the original logs were caulked — with a mixture of manure and mud.

The "long hair and hard hat" work well together, reconstructing the 1887 Royal Canadian Mounted Police barracks, using only the tools of the time. Finished portion of the post is in background.

The museum, centrally located, held a wide variety of
artifacts and a complete history of the town.

Streambed gold was found in the area, but placer mining

Broadax falls and chips fly as another log is squared for fitting. No chain saws were
allowed, and all holes were drilled by hand without benefit of electricity. Fort Steele's
water tower can be seen in the background.

gave way to hydraulic workings. In 1887, Indian trouble developed, and a detachment of seventy-five Northwest Mounted Police arrived, under the leadership of Superintendent Samuel B. Steele, to bring law and order. It was the first Mounty Post west of the Rockies, and the small town once called Galbraith's Ferry, took the name Fort Steele in Sam Steele's honor.

The town hit its peak at the turn of the century, then

Perry Creek water wheel was freighted twenty-five miles to Fort Steele as an example of early utilization of water power in the mining effort.

Oddly roofed outhouse in Fort Steele, B.C., is securely anchored by four posts. Old shops along Main Street are in the background.

faded as the minerals depleted. By 1940 there were only fifty people left in town. It was declared a national historic site in 1961, and reconstruction began.

Although impressive, much of Fort Steele was contrived. But five miles east, some of the original mining equipment remained at a site once called Fisherville, later named Wild Horse.

I found an old shack, a flume, an ancient pickup truck

with a bedstead for a tailgate, and pieces of old mining equipment scattered in all directions. Barren slopes marked the sites of the last hydraulic mining.

And up the hill from the old town, a grave stood surrounded by a battered picket fence. Growing from the center, a huge pine tree offered positive and genuine proof of the grave's antiquity.

Old buildings respond to photographic efforts best during the first and last hours of daylight, when the sun lights the under eaves and throws long shadows to show relief. It was my practice to camp overnight near photogenic sites in order to take advantage of the morning and evening light.

Each morning, after exposing a roll or two, I would con-

It was only a tiny sapling a few years after the child was buried. Now the tree occupies the complete grave site in Wild Horse, B.C.

tinue my travels, on the lookout for a cafe that would offer a big breakfast. In British Columbia that generally means an Oriental cafe. Such cafes offer great Chinese or Japanese food, but most of them consider the cooking of eggs and the brewing of coffee as a compulsory exercise.

Craving good old home cooking, I passed up three or four eating houses with Chinese logos, and finally, late in the morning, I found "Joe's Place." The waitress, a young Chinese girl, took my order, served my coffee, and stood by while I took a sip. Noting my grimace, she explained, "Coffee rouzy." It was — so was the breakfast of burned spuds, dry toast and fried eggs that looked like my grandmother's doilies.

ALBERTA

Nordegg

SO FAR, the Canadian tour had failed to turn up the out-houses, or the stories that I had expected. My next stop was Nordegg, Alberta, just southwest of Edmonton. The usual "well informed" source had convinced me that I should drive the seven hundred extra miles. "It would be worth it," he said.

Nordegg was a provincial prison, and had been for many years. I was stopped at the gate a mile from town. The guard wouldn't consider my request for a guided tour, and got a great laugh out of my reason for requesting it. He did, how-ever, tell me that he had seen — personally — a genuine two-story outhouse in Lundbreck, Alberta.

His tip would have been ignored had not Lundbreck been close to the route home. Calgary was also on the route, but obviously not worth an inquiry. However, I was greatly impressed with the sight of Calgary's bright clean buildings rising out of the plain. Like most Canadian cities, it was re-markably clean, with well groomed parks and nicely kept homes.

Lundbreck

I REACHED LUNDBRECK that evening braced for another disappointment, and indeed, I was once again disappointed.

The two-story outhouse was gone. Don Timmerman, Manager of the LONG HIM General Merchant No. 7, told me the sad story.

The outhouse had been a dandy, with two doors on the upper level, and four on the bottom. At one time it was connected to the Windsor Hotel. The hotel had burned down, leaving the tall outhouse standing alone.

It attracted tourists, so Timmerman bought it for fifteen dollars from one of the partners who had owned the hotel, only to find that the other partner had earlier given the outhouse to the park department in Calgary. I wasn't about to backtrack to Calgary and chance another disappointment.

It was late, so I planned to camp overnight at Lundbreck. In the meantime I could nose about town.

The LONG HIM store has been in continuous operation for seventy-five years, and it still handles merchandise that most would consider antiques, like kerosene stable lanterns and Alladin lamps for the living room. I asked the manager if the No. 7 on the store meant it was one of seven chain stores —

"No, it's just a number."

Next to Store No. 7 are two very old buildings, freshly renovated, and freshly labeled, "Shopping Center — Oldest in the West."

Timmerman was quite surprised to find that other tall

Owner of the Long Him store in Lundbreck, Alberta, bemoaned the loss of the two-story outhouse he purchased as a sales gimmick. He found it had been donated earlier to the Heritage Park in Calgary.

outhouses existed. He had been under the impression that "his" was the only one in the world. He explained that the upper story was reserved for ladies and gentlemen. The lower floor, connected to the hotel bar, was reserved for miners and other less refined folk. He suggested that I stop by in a year or two and have a look at the reconstruction he had planned. It would cost a good deal more than the fifteen dollars he originally planned to invest, but he figured it would be good for business.

Well, I would have to visit Calgary sometime in the future when my enthusiasm returned, and Lundbreck would still be close to the route home.

One year after my visit to Lundbreck, my spirits had revived, and a final plan of attack on the two-story outhouses of Alberta was perfected. The one-year wait was perhaps fortunate, since it gave Calgary a chance to situate its new acquisition, and also Mr. Timmerman of Lundbreck a chance to finish his reconstruction.

In Lundbreck, Alberta, this gas station and store constitute a "shopping center."

Just in case things didn't work out as hoped, I planned to include in the tour a visit to one of my old home towns in Iowa, a look at Flin Flon, Manitoba, and a weeks' fishing in one of my favorite places, La Ronge, Saskatchewan.

My early years of teaching were spent in the small northern Iowa town of Lake Mills. The town was 80 percent Lutheran and 90 percent Norwegian, a combination that allowed no dancing by anyone anywhere, and no drinking or smoking by school teachers. I used to walk three miles into the country to smoke, and would drive fifty miles to buy a beer. The high school coach and I solved the smoking problem by puffing away in the dark recesses of the school's boiler room, where we could use either of two exits. Within a year we had a smokers' group so large we had to elect officers.

Although the town had certain very strict rules, there was no ban on humor. Norwegians enjoy the down-to-earth variety, like the old speaker in the outhouse ploy.

My good friend and hunting partner, Bif (pronounced 'Bife') Bolstad, was one of the prime movers of the stunt. Bif worked at a gas station that offered outside plumbing only. He also had some hell-raising relatives that were mechanically inclined and game for anything. They were the sort to wire your Model A Ford's throttle wide open, or set a mink trap on the floorboards — even put a dead carp under the seat cushion in the heat of summer.

Apparently Bif got his idea about the outhouse speaker from a traveling salesman, and needed only to mention it to his relatives and members of the Saturday night poker gang, of which I was a welcome contributor. In short order, an old radio-record player with attached mike was located. It had been used to announce dances in a nearby town of different ethnic and moral character.

The speaker was stripped out and slung under the seat of the two-holer, and the radio proper hidden behind the outhouse. Finally, a long wire was strung to the mike in the front room of the gas station, right next to the cash register.

We tested it on all of our friends until the word got around town — then we had to pick on strangers. It didn't work so well on the standup traffic, but brought an instant response from the sit-down customers.

We used to sit for hours on weekends waiting for prospects, especially husband and wife combinations. As soon as the wife headed for the outhouse, we would explain to the husband about the mike and loudspeaker. He would always give the go ahead, and get as big a kick as any of us.

As soon as Bif figured the lady was well situated, he'd pick up the mike and say, "Lady, could you move over — I'm working down here and you are in my light!"

The reaction was always outstanding, and when word got out, business increased. Husbands would drive miles to pull a good one on the "old lady."

MANITOBA

Flin Flon

FLIN FLON, MANITOBA is one of a kind. It was named for old Flinerton Flonerty, the leading character in a book owned by one of the early prospectors who searched the area for mineralization.

A number of metals were found in high concentration, and the town that sprouted had to face the immediate problem of building on solid granite, pre–Cambrian bedrock.

Some outhouses were built on elevated cribs, but one man's great idea about combination sewers and sidewalks made a working sewer system possible.

From each house, a sewer pipe ran slightly downhill, surrounded by a long wooden box about four feet square, filled with insulating material. The tops of the long boxes were stoutly planked as elevated boardwalks that seldom needed to be shoveled after a snowfall. The boxes from each house joined trunklines that connected every house and store in town with the sewage plant located at the low point. In some places, where sewers crossed roads, dynamite had been used to penetrate the hard rock.

Outside of town, outhouses were common — so common that prefabricated outhouses, made of particle board, were available at lumber yards.

SASKATCHEWAN

La Ronge

L A RONGE, straight west of Flin Flon, but in the neighboring province of Saskatchewan, did not go the sewer-sidewalk route, although much of the town was built on solid rock. They stayed with the outhouse out back made of particle board, of course.

When I first visited La Ronge a dozen years ago, the street was part gravel and part rounded humps of solid glacier-polished granite. For years there were no flush toilets in town. Then a new government building was constructed, with a septic tank and shiny white porcelain flush stool. Indians, mostly Cree and Chippewa, would travel miles to trip the lever and watch things disappear.

The snowfall in the Northern Plains of Canada was not great enough to warrant tall outhouses, and there was no point in searching about the town. So I went fishing, as planned.

ALBERTA

Calgary

A WEEK LATER I headed south and west for Calgary, looking forward to a visit to Heritage Park, where the two-story outhouse was said to be located.

Heritage Park is big and beautiful, and everything works. The paddlewheel steamer paddles, and the old locomotive makes the rounds. I hurried past a dozen interesting stores to confirm the existence of the tall outhouse.

And there it was in all its glory — a two-door, four-holer on top of a four-door eight-holer, topped with a cupola — and on top of that, blowing in the breeze, the Canadian flag!

It was a dandy. All painted up to match the hotel, with the upper floor connected to the second floor hall by a catwalk, all banistered and beautiful! But the light was wrong — an excuse to look the park over while the sun slowly moved to a more favorable position.

I rode the paddlewheel steamer and watched others scull their shells and paddle canoes. The train spewed coal smoke and blew a steam whistle that brought memories rushing home.

They were baking bread in the bakery, and I ate a slice while watching the smithy shoe a horse. Constable Blake, in Royal Canadian Mounty red, told stories in front of the constabulary. I admired the pelts being baled at the Hudson Bay Fort, and had a sarsparilla in the hotel.

When the light was right, I set about photographing the

Wainwright Hotel of Heritage Park in Calgary, Alberta, was said to have the old Lundbreck two-story outhouse attached to the rear.

two-story outhouse. The flag was missing! It had been placed there as a prank, and I passed up the chance to photograph it. Even without the flag, the outhouse was impressive. It worked — it even smelled!

A plaque at the side explained its history. After the Windsor Hotel in Lundbreck burned down in 1963, Walter Supeta (the other partner) donated the outhouse to the Heritage Park Society.

A few days later, I stood by the reconstructed two-story outhouse in Lundbreck. Don Timmerman had followed the design quite faithfully, but something was lacking. It was a shade too wide, and the lumber was too fresh. The catwalks were missing, and worst of all, it lacked the proper bouquet!

World's finest two-story outhouse, a two-door four-holer over a four-door eight-holer, with a cupola on top. And everything works!

Everything functions in Heritage Park, including stern wheelers and steam engines. You can even sample fresh baked bread from the bakery.

On the long drive home, I considered my long twelve-year search for two-story outhouses and the memorable stories. I was confident that the chore was complete, and looked forward to closing my notebooks, parking my vehicle, and setting to work developing and printing the many negatives I had exposed.

In the mail that had accumulated while I was gone, there was a letter from a Canadian friend by the name of Peter

Byl. He had located a three-story twenty-seat outhouse in Newfoundland!

No matter how many I tracked down, there would al-

Replica of the Hudson Bay Company's Rocky Mountain House has been built on the grounds of Heritage Park.

ways be one more to investigate. This one was too far away, and I had already traveled too far. I would pass on the outhouse in Newfoundland . . . well . . . then again. . . .

Outside of the rebuilt Banff barracks of the Royal Canadian Mounted Police, a constable from years past answers questions and spins a few yarns.

Don Timmerman rebuilt the original Windsor Hotel two-story outhouse quite faithfully. It stands in its original location, minus, of course, the hotel it originally served. Now it serves the public, and brings a few customers into the Long Him Store No. 7.

Index